Scaredy Bat

SERIES COLLECTION: BOOKS 1-3

Scaredy Bat
AND THE FROZEN VAMPIRES

Scaredy Bat
AND THE SUNSCREEN SNATCHER

Scaredy Bat
AND THE MISSING JELLYFISH

By Marina J. Bowman

Illustrated by Yevheniia Lisovaya

This is a work of fiction. Names, characters, places, and incidents either are the product of the author's imagination or are used fictitiously. Any resemblance to actual persons, living or dead, events, or locales is entirely coincidental.

Copyright © 2021 by Code Pineapple

All rights reserved. No part of this book may be reproduced or used in any manner without written permission of the copyright owner except for the use of quotations in a book review.

First paperback edition November 2021

Scaredy Bat and the Frozen Vampires
Written by Marina J. Bowman
Illustrated by Yevheniia Lisovaya

Scaredy Bat and the Sunscreen Snatcher
Written by Marina J. Bowman
Illustrated by Yevheniia Lisovaya

Scaredy Bat and the Missing Jellyfish
Written by Marina J. Bowman
Illustrated by Yevheniia Lisovaya

ISBN 978-1-950341-39-9 (paperback color)
ISBN 978-1-950341-34-4 (paperback black & white)
ISBN 978-1-950341-35-1 (ebook)

Published by Code Pineapple
www.codepineapple.com

For all of you - vampire, human, or otherwise - that have been afraid of something, but didn't let that stop you.

Also by Marina J. Bowman

SCAREDY BAT

A supernatural detective series for kids with courage, teamwork, and problem solving. If you like solving mysteries and overcoming fears, you'll love this enchanting tale!

#1 Scaredy Bat and the Frozen Vampires
#2 Scaredy Bat and the Sunscreen Snatcher
#3 Scaredy Bat and the Missing Jellyfish
#4 Scaredy Bat and the Haunted Movie Set

THE LEGEND OF PINEAPPLE COVE

A fantasy-adventure series for kids with bravery, kindness, and friendship. If you like reimagined mythology and animal sidekicks, you'll love this legendary story!

#1 Poseidon's Storm Blaster
#2 A Mermaid's Promise
#3 King of the Sea
#4 Protector's Pledge

Detective Team

Jessica
"the courage"

Ellie
aka Scaredy Bat
"the detective"

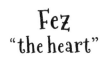

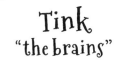

Scaredy Bat
and the Frozen Vampires

By Marina J. Bowman

Illustrated by Yevheniia Lisovaya

Scaredy Bat
AND THE FROZEN VAMPIRES

1. Poof! 01
2. Trenton Academy............................10
3. What Do We Know..........................20
4. Rock, Bat, Dagger 27
5. Shadow on the Horizon 33
6. The Woman in Pink 38
7. The Man in the Photo......................42
8. The Lava Monster............................47
9. Chunky Mummy 51
10. We Have a Problem.........................58
11. Vampire Popsicles............................64
12. The Invisible Message 69
13. Detectives and Heroes.....................76

Batty Bonuses

Are You Afraid of Spiders? 82
Suspect List 84
Who Did It? 89
Hidden Observation Details Sheet 90
Discussion Questions 95

Can you solve the mystery?

All you need is an eye for detail, a sharp memory, and good logical skills. Join Ellie on her mystery-solving adventure by making a suspect list and figuring out who committed the crime! To help with your sleuthing, you'll find a suspect list template and hidden details observation sheets at the back of the book.

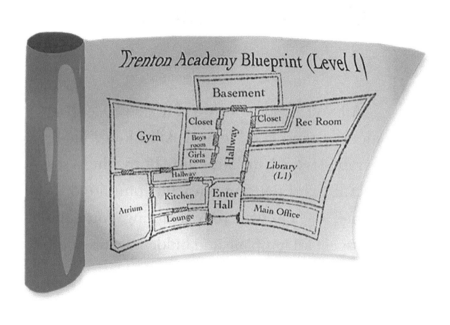

*There's a place not far from here
With strange things 'round each corner
It's a town where vampires walk the streets
And unlikely friendships bloom*

*When there's a mystery to solve
Ellie Spark is the vampire to call
Unless she's scared away like a cat
Poof! There goes that Scaredy Bat*

*Villains and pesky sisters beware
No spider, clown, or loud noise
Will stop Ellie and her team
From solving crime, one fear at a time*

Chapter One
Poof!

Ellie stomped down the hall to her little sister's room only to find pesky Penny nowhere in sight. "Penny!" Ellie cried. "Did you steal my favorite purple dragon necklace?" Ellie dug through the toybox and the closet before laying eyes on Penny's pink coffin bed. She whipped up the sheet to peek underneath, but what she found definitely wasn't her necklace.

Her breath caught in the back of her throat. A hairy spider the size of a watermelon sat just behind the sheet, all eight of his eyes hungrily glaring at Ellie.

"AIYEE!" Ellie shrieked. *POOF!* Just like that she transformed into a bat and flapped into the closet.

"Ha-ha! Got you!" a voice boasted from under the bed. A small girl with straight brown hair and green eyes, much like Ellie's, crawled out from under the coffin bed.

"That's not funny!" Ellie squeaked as she flew out of the closet and transformed back into a vampire. *POOF!*

A large smile spread across Penny's face. "I think it is! It's not my fault you're a big Scaredy Bat. Scaredy Bat! Scaredy Bat! Ellie is a Scaredy Bat!"

Ellie's face grew hot with embarrassment and anger. "Listen, you little brat, when I get my hands on you…" Ellie lunged for her sister, throwing them both onto the pink coffin, where Ellie promptly cocooned Penny in the purple bed sheets before smacking her with a sparkly throw pillow.

"Mom! MOM!" Penny cried.

A woman with curled black hair and a blood-red dress appeared in the bedroom doorway. "What is going on here?" demanded Mom. "Ellie, leave Penny alone!"

Ellie hesitantly backed away from her sister, but not before giving her one more good thwack with the pillow.

Mom stepped up beside Ellie and snatched the pillow. "What is going on?" she asked again.

"She started it!" the two sisters bellowed in unison. Ellie continued, "Penny scared me with… with… THAT." She pointed to the large spider sitting on the floor.

"I just wanted to play! It's not my fault you're scared of everything," sneered Penny.

"It was a giant spider and spiders are gross. How could I not be scared?" Ellie countered.

Suddenly, a purple glimmer in the corner of the room caught Ellie's eye. She whipped her head around to see her sister's favorite bear, Miss Batty. She was wearing the purple necklace!

Ellie raced over and lifted the necklace off the bear. "Another mystery solved by The Great Vampire Detective!" She held up the necklace like an Olympic medal.

Penny snorted. "You have to solve *real* mysteries to be a detective."

Ellie lurched forward for another pillow, but Mom scooped it up before she could get there.

"Okay, that's enough," Mom snapped. "Ellie, you need to finish getting ready or we will be late."

"Why can't I go?" whined Penny, tears pooling in her large eyes.

Mom sighed. "We've already talked about this. No one under twelve can attend the wedding, but don't worry, you'll have a lot more fun with Grandma at the pool today. After all, it is the hottest day of the year."

"Why does Ellie get to go?"

"Because I'm twelve now," Ellie said, beaming. "So, ha!"

"We're lucky that any of us get to go to such an important event," Mom explained. "If your father hadn't performed emergency surgery on King Stanton last year, we wouldn't even be invited."

Before Ellie or Penny could reply, a short

and stout woman with a mixing bowl appeared beside Mom. She looked at Penny, who was still tangled in blankets. "Come on, my Little Fang. I made a batch of fresh blood pudding!"

Penny's eyes grew wide with excitement. "Okay, Grandma!"

Thoughts of the wedding quickly fled and Ellie's mouth watered as she thought about her favorite treat. She loved blood pudding, especially Grandma's since she always made it the best way—extra bloody. "Can I have some pudding, too?" Ellie asked.

Grandma smiled. "Oh, dear, I think you have to go, but I'm sure Penny will save you some."

"No, I won't," Penny proclaimed as she freed herself from the last of the bed sheets. She followed Grandma out into the hall, but not before sticking her tongue out at Ellie.

"Mom, she stuck her tongue out at me!" Ellie complained, prompting Penny to run downstairs.

Mrs. Spark didn't seem to hear her oldest daughter. She fiddled with her wedding rings,

something Ellie knew she only did when she was nervous.

She finally looked over at Ellie. "Did you say something?"

Ellie lied and shook her head.

"Ellie, I need you to be on your best behaviour today. This wedding is very important."

"It's just a fancy wedding," Ellie said.

Mom shook her head. "No, no, it is not. Prince Bennett's brother, Theo, dug up some ancient royal rule yesterday evening, and it turns out that if Bennett doesn't get married by seven o'clock tonight, then the crown falls to Theo. And if Theo gets the crown…" Mom paused as she looked down at her wedding rings. "He will reverse the Fang and Flesh Peace Treaty."

"What does that mean?" Ellie asked.

"That means that any state in the U.S. could choose to make vampire residents illegal again, humans and vampires couldn't get married anymore, and any vampires and humans currently married would be forced to separate."

A lump settled in Ellie's throat, like she

swallowed a golf ball. "You and Dad would have to separate?" Tears stung her eyes as she thought of her vampire Mom and human Dad forced to live apart.

Mom nodded, and her voice softened. "But you don't need to worry about that, love. The wedding is going to be just fine. That is, if we ever get there. Can we go now, please?"

Ellie made her way downstairs as thoughts of her parents separating swirled around her mind. Who would she live with? Would she and Penny live with the same parent? Penny drove her nuts, but she knew she would miss her pesky sister if she didn't get to see her all the time.

As if on cue, Penny excitedly popped in front of Ellie with more blood pudding on her face than in the flowered bowl she held. "Mmm!" she said in an extra loud voice. "This sure is good! Too bad you don't get any."

Okay, maybe Ellie wouldn't miss Penny that much.

"Ellie! Dad is waiting for us in the car. We need to go!" Mom called from across the

house. Ellie rushed out the door, but not before grabbing her favorite turquoise detective coat. She always kept Monster Spray in the pocket, just in case.

Chapter Two
Trenton Academy

The Jotun Frost Giants have made it clear that they favor the end of the Fang and Flesh Peace Treaty and would welcome a vampire king like Prince Theo. This is what their leader had to say—" The sound of the car's radio was replaced by chirping birds as Ellie stepped out of the blue car. The scent of flowers wafted through the air. Ellie and her parents walked up to a towering metal gate that surrounded a large building. With its sun-washed bricks, high arched windows, and glass atrium, the former paper mill's mix of vintage charm and modern beauty was like many of the buildings in Brookside. What was once a remote ghost town in the northern

U.S. known for its failed paper mill was now a thriving community with lush forests, a famous garlic festival, and of course, Trenton Academy.

Trenton Academy was the first school to allow both vampire and human students—even before the Fang and Flesh Peace Treaty—and now it was the chosen venue for the Royal Vampire Wedding.

"*This* is where the Royal Vampire Wedding is?" Ellie asked as she scrunched her nose. "Why would anyone want to have their wedding at a stinky middle school?" While stunning to most with its historical elegance and colorful garden beds, all Ellie could see was a place with mandatory Monday math quizzes and cafeteria food that resembled grey mush.

Dad looked at the secret location that was sent to his phone a mere hour ago. "Yup, this is definitely it."

Mom nudged Ellie and flashed her daughter a look that Ellie knew meant 'behave.' "I'm sure it will be beautiful."

"But why would you get married here when you have a dream palace in the forest?" asked Ellie.

"They wanted it to be a bit more private," answered Dad. "Plus, this school is kind of fitting, since Ayanna is the first human to be married into the Royal Vampire family. Don't you think?"

"I guess," mumbled Ellie. A man in a black suit and a woman in a pink poufy dress distracted Ellie from her disapproval of the venue choice. They stood in the school's attached atrium, holding a piece of paper and small flashlight. *Why do they need a flashlight to read in clear daylight?* Ellie wondered. As the man read to the woman in pink, Ellie tried to read his lips—a detective skill she never seemed to master—while Mom inserted a gold key card into a monitor on the gate.

"GREETINGS!" boomed a robotic voice.

Ellie jumped at the overly loud welcome. "Please standby for a face scan." As a red laser skipped across the trio's faces, Ellie looked back at the atrium, but the couple had disappeared. After a few seconds the voice sounded once

more. "Thank you, Gina Spark, Dr. Harold Spark, and Ellie Spark. You may enter."

Ellie stood with her mouth open as the gate creaked forward. This may be her familiar middle school, but that was definitely new. It was just like a cool piece of tech that her idol, Hailey Haddie, would encounter in her favorite mystery series, *The Amazing Vampire Detective*. She couldn't wait to see what else was inside.

Ellie's amazement grew as they entered the school gym. It no longer looked like the place where smelly boys spilled sweat on the basketball court and gym teachers yelled at her to run faster. Her eyes gleamed as she took in the bright flowers around every corner and elegant ice sculptures in each room. White flowing fabric and twinkle lights hung from the ceiling like sparkly clouds. It looked like a wedding from a fairy tale.

"You made it!" cried a familiar voice behind Ellie.

Ellie turned around to the familiarity of red curls and a bright white, fanged smile. "Jessica!" Ellie gushed. The two girls hugged as if

they hadn't seen each other in weeks, when in reality it had only been a couple days.

"Can you believe this used to be the gym? It looks amazing!" gushed Jessica.

Ellie nodded as she took in more of the stunning decor.

Jessica pointed to a rather poised woman with a light blue dress that perfectly contrasted her tan skin. "That's Shayla Jeffords, the wedding planner," Jessica explained. "My mom said that if she ever gets married again, she would definitely hire Shayla."

Ellie's eyes wandered to Jessica's mom, Camille Perry. Her hair was straight and sleek, unlike her daughter's mess of curls, but those gray-blue eyes were undoubtedly one of the traits that the mother and daughter duo shared, along with their effortless charm that seemed to make everyone like them. Ellie supposed that if you were going to be a big-time actress like Camille Perry, that charm was a must. Ellie refocused on Jessica, who was still chattering on about the wedding.

"…And I hear that some of the food has been specially catered so that it has *never* been tasted before this wedding. Although, I hear they have some frozen desserts, and I don't know how anything will stay frozen for more than a second on the hottest day of the year." Jessica finally caught a breath as she wiped a small bead of sweat from her brow.

"It is super hot today," Ellie said as she tugged at her jacket's collar.

Jessica nodded. "I know. I am so warm. How are you not boiling in that turquoise trench coat?"

Ellie looked down at her long coat. She loved it, but maybe Jessica had a point. She stripped off the jacket, revealing her pink dress and purple stockings with crescent moons. Ellie noted that it wasn't nearly as elegant as Jessica's dark blue dress with subtle sparkles, but she still stood by her choice.

Jessica looked at a nearby air vent and fanned herself with her hand. "Do you want to go outside for a bit?" she asked. "They said they won't start the wedding until the air conditioning kicks in more, so we have a little while."

Ellie nodded. "Sure! Just let me ask my parents." The gym may look nice, but it still felt like the same hot and sticky school Ellie remembered. After her parents agreed, the two girls made their way to the front door just as a short boy in a tux with dark skin and glasses rushed past them.

"Hey, isn't that the boy that had the project that caught last year's science fair on fire?" Ellie whispered.

"I think so," replied Jessica. "On the bright side, it ruined our project, so we automatically got an A."

"That's right!" said Ellie. Both girls laughed.

With the front doors locked, the attached atrium was the closest they could get to outside. It was a quiet space with windowed walls, colorful flowers, and lush greenery. After Ellie and Jessica gushed over the wedding and Ellie complained about her latest fight with Penny, the two friends decided it was time to go back in. As Ellie stood, she plucked a dandelion that was invading one of the pots and blew on the willowy, white seeds. *I wish I could solve a real mystery*, she thought to herself. Just then, she looked up to see Jessica tugging on the glass door, which was sheeted with a sudden, mysterious layer of frost.

Chapter Three
What Do We Know

"The door won't budge!" Jessica exclaimed.

"I think it might be frozen shut," Ellie said, pointing to the ice on the other side of the glass.

With a few more tugs from the duo, the door snapped open and a refreshing cold breeze wisped through the atrium.

"I guess the air conditioning is working now," said Ellie.

"Must be," Jessica agreed.

A piece of paper fluttered down and landed by Ellie's feet.

"What's that?" Jessica asked.

Ellie picked up the sheet, flipped it over a few times, and shrugged. "It's blank."

"Keep it for later!" Jessica insisted. "That way if the wedding is boring, we can pass notes, like we do in class."

Ellie looked down at her pocketless dress and decided to tuck the paper into her shoe.

As the two made their way to the gym, the refreshing breeze soon turned to an aggressive wash of cold that sent both Jessica and Ellie into a shiver frenzy. They peeked through the propped open gym door to find that not only had the air conditioning kicked in, the vents now blew chunky snowflakes throughout the frozen room.

"What happened!?" Jessica shrieked.

Ellie looked at the thick layer of ice that covered almost every surface, including all the guests, who were now frozen statues. Both girls shivered as they took in the snowy scene. "I guess the air conditioning *really* decided to work," Ellie said wearily. Then it dawned on her. "Where are my parents?" Ellie rushed in and found her mom in the back corner—frozen mid-laughter with a wine glass in her hand—while her father stood not much farther with a smile bending up both corners of his lips.

Jessica stood beside her own mother. "Mom. MOM! Can you hear me?" she shouted, but there was no answer.

"We need to call the police," Ellie said.

Jessica nodded. She snapped open her mom's bag and pulled out a small silver phone. She poked at the screen as her teeth began to

chatter. "It's too cold; the touchscreen isn't working. We need to go back to the atrium."

Ellie rubbed her arms. Jessica was right; they couldn't stay here much longer. "I'll get you out of there soon," Ellie whispered to her parents. The two girls raced back to the welcoming warmth of the atrium.

"Here, y-you try d-dialing?" stammered Jessica, still trying to shake off the cold.

Ellie grabbed the phone, and after a few tries, she successfully dialed 9-1-1.

"911, what's your emergency?"

"Everyone is frozen!" Ellie exclaimed.

"Okay, miss. I am going to need more details."

"My friend Jessica and I went inside the atrium at the Royal Vampire Wedding, and when we came back, the whole gym was frozen solid!"

"And where are you?" asked the operator.

"Trenton Academy."

"So, you're at a middle school, which is hosting the royal wedding, and everyone is suddenly frozen on the hottest day of the year?"

"Yes!" confirmed Ellie.

The operator laughed. "Wow, you have one imagination, kid. I'm sorry, but I have to keep this line open for real emergencies, but thanks for giving me a good chuckle." The call ended.

Ellie's mouth gaped in disbelief. "They didn't believe me!"

"What!?" cried Jessica. "But it's true! What do we do now?"

Ellie's stomach did a somersault as she spotted the wish flower that she'd blown on only minutes ago, wishing for a real mystery. A wave of guilt washed over her as she thought about her parents and the ruined wedding's consequences, for them and the rest of the world. She took a deep breath before finally answering, "I think we have to fix this ourselves."

Ellie explained the urgency of the wedding and the consequences if Prince Theo came into power and abolished the Fang and Flesh Peace Treaty.

"That's horrible!" exclaimed Jessica. "So, what should we do first?"

"Well, what do we know? It was super cold in there, almost like a blizzard."

"Which seems nearly impossible on such a hot day," Jessica added as thoughts of the cold gym sent a shiver down her spine.

"And the freezing happened fast. We were just in there and it was still pretty warm, plus everyone that's frozen looks like they were having a good time," Ellie deducted.

"Right." Jessica nodded. "So, what or who could have made that happen?"

"Prince Theo wants the crown, so maybe he did this?"

"But how? It went from boiling to freezing so fast," Jessica said.

"Let's look for clues," suggested Ellie.

Jessica shivered. "Okay, but can we maybe check in here first? I'm still cold."

"Sure," Ellie agreed.

The two girls split up and searched the large atrium. Instantly, Ellie noticed that the atrium's fountain wasn't frozen. So why was the rest of the school so cold? Her eyes wandered to the glass ceiling as a large boot-shaped cloud blew into view.

"Oh my gosh, of course!" Ellie squealed.

"What?" Jessica asked eagerly.

"A Jotun Frost Giant did this," Ellie replied.

Jessica's eyes grew wide. "A what?"

"Yeah, a what?" came a voice from behind them.

Chapter Four
Rock, Bat, Dagger

The two girls jumped, and *POOF!*, Ellie transformed into a bat and darted into a nearby tree.

Beside a wooden bench stood a stocky boy in an apron licking a dripping ice cream cone. He looked at Ellie in the tree as trails of vanilla and chocolate made their way down his arm. "Wow, that's awesome!" he marveled.

"Who are you?" demanded Jessica.

POOF! "Yeah, what she said," added Ellie, now back in her vampire form.

The boy licked a run of ice cream that streamed down his arm. "Fizz," he said as he slurped up the last drip.

"Fizz?" questioned Ellie. "What kind of name is that?"

The boy laughed as he shoved the last of his cone into his mouth and wiped his hands on his apron. "Fez, not Fizz," he explained after he swallowed the last of his treat.

"Wait a second," said Jessica, "don't you go to our school?"

Fez nodded. "Yup, I recognize you two." He held out his hand. "It's nice to officially meet you!"

Jessica and Ellie both looked down at the boy's chubby fingers, still visibly covered in melted ice cream. Not wanting to be rude, they both accepted the sticky handshake and introduced themselves.

"My Dad is catering the wedding," Fez said. "I was helping him get the food ready in the cafeteria kitchen when suddenly a huge blast of cold air and snow shot through the school!"

"I knew it!" boasted Ellie. "I knew it had to have been sudden."

Jessica, however, didn't share in Ellie's excitement. "Hey Fez," said Jessica, "if you were inside

like you claim to be, then why didn't you freeze?"

Fez shrugged. "I was wondering that too, but I figure it must have been because I have so much of my dad's secret hot sauce on me. It gives off a ton of heat!"

Jessica and Ellie glanced at each other, both thinking it was an unlikely story.

"There is no way a sauce could give off that much heat," Ellie spat.

"See for yourself," insisted Fez. He handed a small bag of thick, red sauce to Ellie. It did feel warm, but how could it give off enough heat for someone not to be flash-frozen?

"It's not *that* hot," Ellie said matter-of-factly.

Fez snickered. "If you don't think it's hot, try some."

Ellie looked at Jessica. "Rock, Bat, Dagger to see who tries it?"

Jessica rolled her eyes and sighed. "Fine," she agreed.

The two girls stretched out their hands and chanted, "Rock, Bat, Dagger." Ellie's hand landed in the shape of a dagger and Jessica's in a rock-shaped fist.

"Ha! Rock beats dagger," Jessica said.

Ellie took a deep breath before squirting a large dollop onto her finger. "Well, here goes nothing," she gulped. She licked the warm goop off her finger and swished it around her mouth.

"Maybe you should have had a smaller taste," said Fez.

"Why?" asked Ellie. "This is—this is—oh my gosh! My mouth is on FIRE!" Ellie stuck out her tongue and panted like a dog.

Jessica looked over at Fez, who chuckled as Ellie ran around the atrium. "I'm going to say that your story checks out," chortled Jessica.

Fez's smile widened. "I'm glad, because it's the truth."

Ellie ran back over with her eyes watering and her tongue still hanging out. "That is the hottest thing I have ever tasted." She licked her lips. "It is quite tasty, though."

"Hey guys, earlier you said something about a Jelly Frost Giant? Is that some sort of snack? It sounds delicious!" said Fez.

Ellie laughed. "Jotun Frost Giant. They're not a snack, they're these huge giants that live in the mountains, but when they come out, they create freakish blizzards and freeze things."

"That sure does sound like what happened here." Jessica shuddered.

Fez gulped. "You think one did this?"

"When I was getting out of the car today, I heard on the radio that the Jotun Frost Giants would welcome a vampire king like Prince Theo. And they definitely have the power to freeze the school this fast."

Ellie looked around the atrium and raced to a corner under a bench. "Aha!" she exclaimed. "Proof that the Frost Giants were here."

Chapter Five
Shadow on the Horizon

Ellie held up a grey ball of fluff. "Sometimes they ride giant wolves, and this definitely looks like wolf fur," she exclaimed.

Jessica and Fez ran over to get a better look at the clue. Jessica squinted as she examined the find. "You sure that's wolf fur?" she asked.

"It does kind of look like a big dust bunny," Fez said.

Ellie's proud smile quickly faded. "Well, I guess the wolf fur wouldn't be in here, since this part of the school isn't frozen. But maybe it blew in through the vents?"

The three looked around the room only to find no vents in sight.

Ellie dropped the grey dust bunny to the ground and wiped her hands on her dress. "There are really no cold mountains around here, though, and I doubt a Frost Giant would come all this way."

"Plus, I don't think they would risk angering the rest of the royal family," Jessica added.

Ellie's eyes grew wide. "But if Frost Giants didn't do this, what is that!" She pointed to a shadow on the horizon outside before *POOF!* She raced back into the nearby tree.

Fez and Jessica looked to where Ellie had pointed. "Ellie, all I see is a blue sky," Jessica said, perplexed.

"Me, too," agreed Fez.

POOF! Ellie popped back down from the tree and looked over at the spot where the giant's silhouette stood. "It's right there!" she cried.

Jessica looked at the spot and then over at Ellie. "Oh, Ellie." She laughed. She took Ellie's glasses off and wiped the lenses on her dress. "Here, now look again," Jessica said, handing Ellie her glasses.

Ellie put on her glasses, and felt her face grow hot. "Oh," she mumbled.

Fez chuckled. "So, Frost Giants are glasses smudges. Good to know."

Ellie put her hand on her hips. "No! Jotun Frost Giants live in cold, mountainous environments and can be super evil with their icy powers." She took her hands off her hips. "But I don't think they did this."

"What is sticking out of your shoe?" asked Fez.

Ellie pulled out the folded sheet. "Just a piece of blank paper we found in here earlier." Suddenly, she remembered the couple reading the paper in the atrium when she was at the gate. "We need to find the woman in a pink and poufy dress that I saw reading in the atrium with a man in a suit," she said. "I think this is written in invisible ink, so we need the special flashlight thing to read it, and she might have it."

"Oh, just like the jungle episode of *The Amazing Vampire Detective* where Hailey Haddie needs to send a secret note?" asked Fez.

"Exactly!" said Ellie.

Chapter Six
The Woman in Pink

Once again, they made their way into the frosty school. The biting cold nipped at every inch of them as they entered the gym. Ellie peeled her turquoise trench coat from where she left it and began searching for the pink dress. Everything was frozen. Even the photos of the royal couple had small icicles hanging from the frames. Ellie spotted a frozen woman wearing a puffy pink dress and a mean scowl on her face. What was she holding?

"Guys, I think I found her!" Ellie shouted.

Fez rushed over, and Ellie pointed to the woman.

"Hey, I recognize her," said Fez. "Earlier today I overheard her bragging about how

much better of a princess she would have made. Do you think she might be behind this?"

"Maybe she is jealous of Bennett marrying Ayanna and did this to ruin the wedding," offered Ellie. "But is that a wedding ring on her finger?"

"Yup," Jessica confirmed as she arrived. "She is married. My mom actually knows her. Her name is Talia, and she is Prince Bennett's ex-girlfriend. Although she is absolutely full of herself, I don't think she could have done this." She pointed to Talia's finger. "She's married, she's frozen, and not to sound mean, but I don't think she is clever enough."

Fez snickered. "Well, now that you mention it, she did mistake the kitchen area for the girl's washroom and repeatedly tried to pull open the door, even though it clearly says 'push'."

"Yup, that's definitely her," Jessica confirmed.

"But what about this?" Ellie said, pointing to the cylindrical, black item Talia held. She answered her own question, spotting a large moustache drawn on Ayanna's portrait.

"Are you going to bother giving someone a marker moustache if you plan to freeze their whole wedding?" Fez asked.

"Probably not," Ellie agreed. "I thought she was holding what we need to read the invisible ink."

"Her art does look pretty funny though," Jessica said, taking a few photos of the moustached photo with her mom's phone. As the biting cold intensified, the two girls could no longer fight off their shivers. "Let's check the lost-and-found for some warmer clothes," Jessica suggested.

Ellie tried to warm her hands with her breath. "That's a great idea!" she agreed.

The trio went to the nearby lost-and-found to find the bin that usually overflowed with mismatched mittens, scratchy scarves, and long forgotten coats nearly empty.

Fez reached in and picked up a frayed set of headphones, an oversized pink ruler, and a silver compact mirror. "Unless these can somehow keep a vampire warm, I don't think they will help."

Both girls huddled together as their shivering intensified. Ellie looked over at Fez searching through another bin in nothing but a t-shirt, apron, and shorts. How was he not cold?

Chapter Seven
The Man in the Photo

"Aha!" Looking down at Fez's bulging pockets, Ellie found her answer. "Fez, do you have any extra hot sauce?" she asked.

"Is now really the time to think about your hunger?" Jessica snapped.

"No, Jess. Look how warm he is with that hot sauce in his pockets."

Jessica looked over at Fez. "Of course, that's why he's still warm. Just like how he avoided getting flash-frozen." Not only wasn't he shivering like Ellie and Jessica, but he even seemed to be sweating slightly.

Fez turned around to address Ellie's question. "Sure, there's lots in the kitchen. I'll be right back!" He bolted out of the room.

Jessica gave off a big shiver and looked over at Ellie. "Fez is really nice," she said. "When this is all over, we should definitely hang out with him."

"Definitely!" Ellie agreed. She looked up at the clock. *6:15*. They were running out of time.

"While we're waiting, I've been meaning to ask you. Do you want my yellow dress with the green flowers?" Jessica asked.

Although Ellie's mind was still in detective mode, she indulged her friend. "Which one is that again?"

"Hold on, I think my mom has a pic on her phone." Jessica opened the phone to the photo of the moustached Ayanna.

Who was that in the photo with her? Ellie thought. Jessica began to swipe past the photo. "Wait, go back!" Ellie said. Her eyes grew wide as she recognized that brown hair and face. "That's him! Prince Theo is the man that I saw with Talia in the atrium. We need to find him."

Fez rushed in holding big bags of sauce and a men's dress jacket. He dropped everything

in a heap by the door before bending over to catch his breath.

"I thought you could use something with pockets for the sauce," said Fez, looking up at Jessica. He picked up a black men's dress coat and handed it to her. "This probably isn't your size, but it will help keep you warm."

Jessica graciously took the jacket. "Then I'm on board!" she said. The hem fell to her knees and the sleeves had to be rolled numerous times, but it did the trick.

"We need to find Prince Theo," Ellie told Fez. "He's the one I saw with Talia in the atrium reading the secret note."

They ventured to the gym, determined and warm. After looking around for several minutes, they couldn't spot Theo anywhere. *Where could he be?* Ellie wondered.

Just then the room went black, and the silhouette of a large monster appeared in the doorway.

Chapter Eight
The Lava Monster

*P*OOF! Ellie fluttered under the table and Jessica dived after her. Ellie's heart sat in her throat as she saw what could only be described as a glowing lava monster inching closer to the tablecloth. Its hand reached for the white linen and flipped up the fabric to reveal the terrifying face of… Fez?

"Fez! What happened?" Jessica asked. "And why are you glowing?"

Fez looked down at the bright red glow coming from his pockets before focusing back on Jessica. "Someone or something turned off the lights, and you're glowing, too!"

Jessica looked down at her glowing pockets. Fez was right! She reached in and pulled out

a squishy bag of sauce from her jacket pocket. Sure enough, it was the spicy concoction that gave off the warm glow.

"Did you see who it was?" Jessica asked.

Fez shrugged. "Nope, I couldn't make out much." He pulled Jessica out from under the table.

POOF! Ellie appeared next to them.

"We need to find out who turned off the lights," insisted Jessica. "I bet they're behind this!"

Ellie and Fez agreed, and they headed toward the door. Ellie arrived first and gave the handle a big tug, but the metal door wouldn't budge.

"Don't be like Talia. Try pushing," suggested Jessica.

Ellie tried pushing, but it still wouldn't move. They all tried to push and pull, but the door was frozen shut. After five minutes of effort, the trio slunk to the floor.

"What now?" asked Ellie. Neither of the others had an answer.

The silence of the gym was soon filled with a loud crunching. The girls looked over to see Fez snacking on a plate of what looked like

chips topped with purple mashed potatoes. "Want some?" he asked.

Ellie and Jessica both shook their heads.

"You sure? It's extra delicious with the hot sauce." Fez squeezed out a thick dollop of red sauce onto a chip before shoving it in his mouth.

"That's it!" announced Ellie as she sprang to her feet. "Fez, I need some hot sauce."

Fez looked down longingly at the bag he'd planned to use on his chips before handing it to Ellie.

Quickly, Ellie opened a corner and dripped some of the sauce on the cracks of the door. It hissed and sizzled until the door crackled free of the frost's icy clutch. Once in the hallway there was light, but no sign of anyone.

"Where do you think the monster went?" asked Ellie.

"Maybe it went— WOAH!" Suddenly Fez crashed to the ground.

"Are you okay?" Jessica and Ellie asked in unison.

Fez rubbed his elbow. "Yeah, I just slipped on this ice."

Ellie looked down at the stream of ice that trailed all the way from the gym down the hall. "If we find where this ice trail goes, I bet we'll find the monster. Fez, Jessica, let's follow that trail!"

Chapter Nine
Chunky Mummy

They tracked the ice trail all the way to the maintenance room in the basement. Ellie pressed her ear to the door, and sure enough, heavy breathing and monsterly sounds came from inside.

Ellie gulped. "Maybe we should wait until they come out. It's probably just Prince Theo behind this anyway. Right?"

"It looked more like a monster to me," said Fez.

"Some vampires can transform into creatures, so maybe Theo is one. Whoever it is, we need to get them to tell us how to fix this," Jessica said.

Jessica pointed to her watch. "We're running out of time. We need to do this now. Ready? On the count of three. One, two, three." On three, they flung open the door, catching a chunky-looking mummy by surprise. The mummy sprang from the dark corner and tried to dash away, but the team tackled him to the ground.

Ellie pulled her special monster spray from her pocket and gave him a good spritz. "Ha, we got you now, Mr. Monster!" Ellie roared.

The cushy mummy rolled around the floor and grumbled in monster language. That is, until he suddenly spoke perfect English. "Wait, guys. WAIT!" pleaded the mysterious fiend. "I'm Tink. My foster mom is the wedding planner, Shayla Jeffords. I was just trying to help her out when everything went terribly wrong. Please don't spray me again with…" Tink let out a couple coughs. "Is that lavender spray?"

Ellie's face grew hot. "No! It's not lavender spray… It's lavender *monster* spray."

Tink stuck out his tongue in disgust. "Well, either way, it tastes terrible," he replied.

Ellie beamed. "Good, then it works!"

Tink unpeeled a few of the layers of the clothing that engulfed him.

"What are you wearing?" Jessica asked.

"I grabbed some stuff from the lost and found," Tink said as he struggled to pull a sweater over his head. "I needed something to stay warm after I accidentally supercharged the air conditioning system."

"Supercharged the air conditioner? How?" Fez asked.

"And why?" Ellie added.

Tink sighed. "I was just trying to help Ms. Jeffords cool down the wedding. Now everyone is frozen and I can't figure out how to fix it. I supercharged the air conditioner using this special device I invented, but it worked too well." Tink pointed to what looked like a contraption made with a garbage can, vacuum cleaner, and an ice sculpture. "I tried to thaw everything by

turning on the heat. I even turned off all the lights around the building to get more power, but it still isn't warm enough."

"That ice trail must be where you dragged the ice sculpture," concluded Ellie.

"And that's why you turned the lights out on us," added Fez.

"Oops, sorry," mumbled Tink. "I didn't know there was anyone not frozen." Tink looked at the unfrozen trio. "Um, why aren't you guys frozen? I thought everywhere in the school froze, except here since there are no vents."

"Ellie and I were in the atrium," Jessica answered. "There aren't any vents in there, either."

Tink squinted at the blueprint of the school that sat on the table. "Oh, you're right!" Tink then looked at Fez. "Why didn't *you* freeze?"

"I had this," said Fez. He took a bag of hot sauce out of his pocket and plopped it on the desk.

Tink looked down at the red bag with raised eyebrows. "Because you have spaghetti sauce?" he asked.

"It's hot sauce," explained Ellie. "And it has super-heating powers. When you turned off the lights and closed the door, the door froze shut, but this stuff unfroze it."

A wide grin stretched across Tink's face. "How much sauce do you guys have?"

"I have a few bags here," replied Fez, "and there's a big pot of it in the kitchen. Plus, there are a few extra-large bags I hid in the kitchen vent for a snack later, but your supercharged air conditioning blew them too far down to reach."

"If you guys can get me that pot, I can supercharge the heating system and thaw everything. I know you guys don't know me, but—"

"We're here to help!" Ellie declared.

"We don't want to see the royal wedding ruined anymore than you do," Jessica assured.

"What they said," Fez chimed in.

Tears glazed Tink's eyes. "Thanks, guys."

The team quickly introduced themselves and drew up a plan. Tink reached inside his backpack, which seemed to have everything from gadgets to gum. He handed out walkie talkies to Ellie, Jessica, and Fez.

They knew what they had to do.

Chapter Ten
We Have a Problem

An icy blast of air sent a shiver through Ellie as she pushed open the girls' changing room. "Hello? Helloooooo?" Ellie called, but no one answered. As she rounded the corner, she found the soon-to-be princess, Ayanna, and all her bridesmaids still frozen. While everyone else in the building seemed to be slowly thawing, this bunch looked as if they hadn't started to melt at all.

Ellie crept closer to Ayanna. Even frozen, she was more beautiful than Ellie had imagined with her smooth, dark skin and voluminous curls—both still radiant even while covered in a thick layer of ice. Another shiver

surged down Ellie's spine. Why was it still so cold in here?

She walked around the room searching for the vent, but all she found were ice sculptures and flowers masking the plain brick walls of the changing room. Ellie pulled out her walkie talkie. "Umm, guys. We have a problem. The princess' dressing room isn't getting any heat, and I can't find a vent anywhere."

Tink's voice sounded on the radio. "The blueprints say that there should be a vent in the opposite corner to the door."

"Okay, I'll check," said Ellie. A large, heart-shaped ice sculpture sat in the spot that Tink had described. Upon closer inspection, Ellie noticed a vent, but not only was the sculpture completely blocking any air flow, it had fused itself to the metal cover. Ellie leaned into the ice sculpture, her feet slipping as she pushed with all her might.

"Did you find it?" asked Tink over the radio.

"I did, but there is an ice sculpture blocking it and it won't move!" Ellie answered.

"You're going to have to melt it, Ellie."

Ellie reached into her pocket and palmed the small bag of sauce. Not nearly enough to get through that huge block. "I don't have enough sauce," she replied.

"Well, you know where there is more…" Fez chimed in.

"No way! NO WAY!" Ellie cried. "I am not crawling into a vent to get those extra bags. There are spiders and bugs in there."

"Ellie!" Jessica called. "This could be the difference between saving the wedding or not. I'm busy setting up the atrium, Tink is dealing with the vents, and Fez is in the kitchen. You have to do it."

"I can't do it!" Ellie sulked.

"Think of your parents and what might happen if Theo takes the crown," begged Jessica. "What if he makes all vampire and human marriages illegal and they're forced to separate?"

Ellie's nostrils flared. She wasn't going to let that happen. She looked over at Ayanna and

pulled the walkie talkie back up to her mouth. "Fine! I'll do it."

"I'll make sure the air is turned off in that part of the school," Tink exclaimed.

Ellie stuffed the device into her coat pocket as cheers of encouragement from the others rang through the monitor. She rushed out the door and rounded the corner to the nearest vent. Squatting down, she carefully popped off the vent cover. With a quick stretch to the left and then to the right, *POOF!* She shrank into a bat and flapped through the metal shaft. Cobwebs coated her wings and the distinct smell of bugs filled her nostrils.

"Ew! Ew! Ew!" shrieked Ellie.

She flapped on and saw a glow farther down the tunnel. The sauce! Ellie's eyesight admittedly wasn't great when she became a bat, but was that a small, glowing bag scurrying towards her? A plump spider that clearly enjoyed the sauce scuttled down the vent, bringing Ellie to a screeching halt—literally. She

yelled at the top of her lungs, so much so that when she went to take a breath, she inhaled the spider!

Chapter Eleven
Vampire Popsicles

Cough! Cough! Crunch! Ellie accidentally bit down on the squishy creature and was greeted with a burst of flavor. A flavor both sweet and spicy, no doubt thanks to Fez's father's secret hot sauce. That spider was delicious!

Ellie's fear subsided. Could she really be afraid of something so tasty? She continued to cruise through the vent, lapping up every insect she could find. Even the ones that weren't stuffed with the sauce were a crunchy delight. Soon she found the real bags of sauce and grabbed two with her feet before flapping out the nearest vent.

POOF! "I've got the sauce!" she called into the walkie talkie. She raced into the dressing

room and poured the sauce on the statue. The ice sizzled and hissed—melting down into nothing but a puddle—and hot air poured in through the vent.

Ellie looked at frozen Ayanna on the other side of the room and then at her watch. *6:50.* Only ten minutes left for the wedding to

happen, and Ayanna wasn't going to thaw in time. Ellie squished the last big bag of sauce in her hand. She knew what she had to do.

With one big splat, the whole bag of red sauce coated Ayanna's icy exterior, and with a couple sizzles and crackles, she was free.

"What happened?" Ayanna cried. She looked over at her frozen bridesmaids and gasped. "Why are they vampire popsicles?!"

Ellie giggled. "I'll explain later! You need to go get married!" Ellie grabbed the princess' hand and rushed her to the atrium. The last of the chairs were being set up, and the sun started to set. It was still humid and muggy in there, but no one seemed to mind.

Prince Bennett arrived seconds later. "Ayanna! Are you okay?" he asked, his eyes trailing down to Ayanna's once-white gown, now splattered in red. "What's on your dress?"

Ayanna looked down, noticing the splash of color on her dress for the first time. "Umm, I'm not sure."

"It's sauce," Ellie chimed in. "It actually goes really well with spiders!"

The couple stared at Ellie blankly, but before either of them could ask any more questions, a man ushered them to the altar.

"There you are!" cried a familiar voice. Ellie turned to see her parents rushing toward her.

"Mom! Dad!" Ellie cried as she ran over to give them a hug.

Mrs. Spark reached down to a splotch on Ellie's shoulder, worry lines crinkled her still-perfect makeup. "Are you bleeding? Did you get hurt?"

Ellie looked over at the spot and laughed. "No, Mom. I'm fine."

Dad swabbed the sauce with his finger, rubbing it between his index and his thumb. "Just as I suspected, not blood." He licked his finger. "Wow! That is super spicy." Mr. Spark's face turned red as he let out a couple coughs.

"Will everyone please have a seat?" said a tall man beside the royal couple. "We need to start this wedding."

Chapter Twelve
The Invisible Message

After a quick wedding and a whole lot of explaining, Ellie took a seat at a reception table with her oldest friend, her two newest friends, and Prince Bennett.

"I just wanted to thank you all for saving the wedding," Bennett said. "I don't want to think about what would have happened without your quick thinking. Enjoy the reception, and let me know if you ever need anything." Before he walked away, the folded piece of paper that stuck out of Ellie's shoe caught his eye. "Are those my vows?" he asked.

Ellie pulled the paper out of her shoe. "I don't think so. I found this blank piece of paper in the atrium. I think it has invisible ink."

Prince Bennett smiled and pulled the flashlight-like device out of his pocket. "You are quite the detective, Ellie Spark." He shone the colored light on the paper to reveal a mess of handwriting.

"But why did your brother have it?" asked Ellie.

Bennett shrugged. "Probably his way of trying to stop the wedding. I also found him earlier in the library with this," he wiggled the small light, "so I'm not surprised." Ellie handed the vows over, and the prince went on his way.

"Hey Ellie, I have a question," said Fez in a hushed voice.

"Okay," said Ellie.

"What's it like to be able to turn into a bat?"

Ellie shuffled uncomfortably in her seat. She had been so caught up in the investigation that she didn't even realize that Fez wasn't a vampire. All her friends had always been just like her, and even though she interacted with plenty of humans at school and in town, she had never spent this much time with one. "It's

pretty cool," she answered, "except I can't control it all the time. Like when I get scared, it just kind of happens… that's why some people call me Scaredy Bat."

"I think it's super cool!" reassured Fez. "Before we moved here, we lived in a town that didn't allow vampires, so I don't know much about them."

"Can I ask you a question?" asked Ellie.

Fez nodded.

"Are you afraid of me at all because I'm a vampire?"

Fez paused for a moment before answering, "Nah, my parents have made friends with plenty of vampires since we moved here. But they never let me ask them questions and I have soooo many."

"Well, I'd be glad to answer some," Ellie said.

Tink popped his head into the conversation. "I have a question. Do you actually drink blood? All the textbooks say you do, but I just can't imagine."

"Oh, that's a good one! If you do drink blood, is it human blood?" asked Fez.

"And if so, where do you get it?" added Tink as he lifted his collar to hide his exposed neck.

Ellie began to sweat. She had never been asked so many questions about being a vampire before, or any for that matter, so she wasn't sure where to start.

Fez and Tink eagerly waited for Ellie's answer, but they were only met with silence.

Jessica giggled. "Guys, I think you're overwhelming her. It's true, ancient vampires used to go around biting necks and sucking blood."

Both boys lost all color in their faces as their skin flushed a ghostly white.

"But we don't do that anymore. That's so out of fashion," Jessica explained. "Now we pretty much eat whatever we want, although many of us still eat mostly meat. But stuff like humans would, like steak and chicken."

"And we are really drawn to red food." Ellie added, finally finding her words. "My Dad says it's because our brains associate the color with

meal time. I love red licorice! But black licorice is super gross." She scrunched her nose as she pictured the black candy.

Tink and Fez let out sighs of relief. "Well, blood drinkers or not, I think you guys are all awesome!" exclaimed Tink. "Thank you so much for helping me today. You're great detectives." He paused for a moment before adding, "I wish I could solve mysteries like you guys."

"You can!" exclaimed Ellie without missing a beat.

Tink looked down at the ground. "But what help can I be? I almost ruined today. You guys are the ones that saved the wedding."

"We couldn't have done it without your quick thinking to put the sauce in your machine," Jessica said. "Anything we did to thaw the wedding would have made it too late!"

Tink smiled slightly. "Well, I wouldn't have been able to do it without Fez's hot sauce. That stuff packs quite the punch."

"I just thought it was delicious. Ellie is the one who discovered it could melt things," said Fez.

"And I would have never had the courage to get the rest of the sauce to save Ayanna without Jessica," explained Ellie. She looked across the table at her three smiling friends and Ellie couldn't help but smile, too. "I think we make a pretty great team!"

Chapter Thirteen
Detectives and Heroes

"*Right before the clock struck seven, Ayanna and Prince Bennett were married. If the ceremony had taken place mere moments later, the prince would have had to renounce his crown, but this story has a happy ending. The Royal Vampire Wedding was saved, all thanks to these four middle school kids: Tink Taylor, Jessica Perry, Fez Fitzgerald, and Ellie Spark. If you ask us, our small town has quite the group of detectives and heroes on our hands!*" said the reporter.

The four detectives proudly beamed and waved at the camera.

"*This is Kelly Anders for Channel 5 News. Back to you, Karl.*"

Ellie flicked off the TV and smiled at her sister.

Penny's mouth sat wide open as she stared at the now-blank TV. "I can't believe that you saved the day. You're a big Scaredy Bat."

"Well, maybe I'm not anymore."

Penny laughed. "Yeah, right! You are too."

Ellie shrugged and yawned. "Anyway, I've

had a big day, so I'm going to bed." She headed upstairs and pulled back the sheets in her coffin, revealing a surprise bedmate.

As the hairy, eight legs inched their way towards Ellie, Penny smirked in the doorway. "What are you going to do, Scaredy Bat?"

Ellie picked up the spider by one of its legs, opened her mouth, and plopped it right onto her tongue.

Penny's eyes widened, and her face turned a sickly green.

Ellie swallowed and licked her lips. "Delicious!"

Penny raced the other way. "Mom! MOM!" she cried.

Ellie giggled. Maybe she *wasn't* a Scaredy Bat anymore.

Just then a crack of thunder shook the house, and *POOF!* Ellie flew under her bed.

Okay, so maybe she was still a *little* bit of a Scaredy Bat. But Scaredy Bats make the best detectives.

Are You Afraid of Spiders?

Arachnophobia is the extreme or irrational fear of spiders and other eight-legged arachnids (like scorpions). Arachnophobia comes from the Greek word for spider, which is "arachne," and "phobos," the Greek word for fear.

Fear Rating: Arachnophobia is one of the top 10 most common phobias in the world. People with this phobia usually get panic attacks, faint, sweat excessively, cry, or scream at the sight of spiders.

Origin: Fear of spiders is an evolutionary response, and developed from the association between spiders and diseases in the past.

- Most spiders are not harmful to humans. They only bite in self-defense, and have no more effect than a mosquito bite.
- Only 2 kinds of spiders in the U.S. are venomous to people: the black widow and brown recluse.
- In the world, only 25 species of spiders can harm humans, out of about 40,000.
- Spiders eat over 2,000 insects a year, preventing our homes and gardens from being overrun with flies and mosquitoes.
- Some cultures, such as native Americans, believe that spiders bring good luck and are seen as a symbol of wisdom.
- Fried spiders are a crunchy treat in some places, including Cambodia. DO NOT eat spiders without parent supervision!

Fear No More! Spiders do more good than harm. But if you believe you suffer from arach-nophobia and want help, talk to your parents or doctor about treatment options. For more fear facts, visit: scaredybat.com/bundle1.

Suspect List

Fill in the suspects as you read, and don't worry if they're different from Ellie's suspects. When you think you've solved the mystery, fill out the "who did it" section on the next page!

Name: Write the name of your suspect

Motive: Write the reason why your suspect might have committed the crime

Access: Write the time and place you think it could have happened

How: Write the way they could have done it

Clues: Write any observations that may support the motive, access, or how

Suspect 1

Draw below

Name:
Motive:
Access:
How:
Clues:

Suspect 2

Draw below

Name:	
Motive:	
Access:	
How:	
Clues:	

Suspect 3

Draw below

Name:
Motive:
Access:
How:
Clues:

Suspect 4

Draw below

Name:
Motive:
Access:
How:
Clues:

Who Did It?

Now that you've identified all of your suspects, it's time to use deductive reasoning to figure out who actually committed the crime! Remember, the suspect must have a strong desire to commit the crime (or cause the accident) and the ability to do so.

For more detective fun, visit:
scaredybat.com/bundle1

Name:	
Motive:	
Access:	
How:	
Clues:	

Hidden Details Observation Sheet
-- Level One --

1. What did Ellie find hidden under her sister Penny's bed?
2. What kind of animal does Ellie turn into?
3. Where did Ellie find her necklace at the beginning of the book?
4. What is Ellie's favorite snack?
5. What does Ellie always keep in the pocket of her detective coat?
6. Where did the royal vampire wedding take place?
7. Where were Ellie and Jessica when everyone else froze?
8. What did Fez have that prevented him from freezing?
9. What kind of monster appeared in the doorway when the lights went out?
10. Why didn't Tink freeze?

Hidden Details Observation Sheet
-- Level Two --

1. What kind of necklace does Ellie wear?
2. What is the name of Penny's favorite stuffed bear?
3. What is the name of Ellie's school?
4. Who did Ellie see talking in the atrium when she first arrived at the wedding?
5. What was Fez eating when he first met Ellie and Jessica?
6. What did Ellie find that made her think the Jotun Frost Giants did it?
7. What was Talia holding in her frozen hand?
8. By what time did Prince Bennett and Ayanna need to be married?
9. What scent is Ellie's monster spray?
10. What was written on the paper Ellie found with invisible ink?

Hidden Details Observation Sheet
-- Level Three --

1. Who is Penny's favorite celebrity?
2. What was the minimum age to attend the royal vampire wedding?
3. Why did Ellie's family get invited to the wedding?
4. What sits on the shelf above the TV in Ellie's house?
5. Where does Ellie's grandfather appear in the story? (hint: he has a mustache and detective hat)
6. Who is Shayla Jeffords?
7. What does Jessica's mom do for work?
8. What is the name of Fez's family's restaurant?
9. What kind of ice sculpture was blocking the vent in the girls dressing room?
10. Who does Ellie have a poster of in her room?

For more detective fun, visit:
scaredybat.com/bundle1

Level One Answers

1. A spider
2. A bat
3. On Penny's stuffed bear
4. Blood pudding
5. Monster Spray
6. Ellie's school
7. The atrium
8. Hot sauce
9. Lava Monster aka Fez
10. No vents in the basement

Level Two Answers

1. Purple dragon necklace
2. Miss Batty
3. Trenton Academy
4. Talia and Theo
5. An ice cream cone
6. A gray ball of fluff
7. A black marker
8. Seven o'clock
9. Lavender
10. Prince Bennett's vows

Level Three Answers

1. Silvia Romez
2. Twelve
3. Her dad performed surgery on King Stanton
4. A crystal egg
5. A framed picture in the living room
6. Tink's foster mom and the wedding planner
7. Acting
8. Hudson Heat
9. A heart-shaped ice sculpture
10. Hailey Haddie

Answer Key

Discussion Questions

1. What did you enjoy about this book?
2. What are some of the major themes of this story?
3. Who was your favorite character? What did you like about him/her?
4. Is the setting important to the book? In what ways?
5. How are Ellie, Jessica, Fez, and Tink similar? How are they different? How did they help each other in the story?
6. If you could turn into a certain type of animal whenever you wanted, what kind of animal would you choose? Why?
7. What fears did the characters express in the book? When have you been afraid? How have you dealt with your fears?
8. What other books, shows, or movies does this story remind you of?
9. What do you think will happen in the next book in the series?
10. If you could talk to the author, what is one question you would ask her?

ScaredyBat

and the Sunscreen Snatcher

By Marina J. Bowman

Illustrated by Yevheniia Lisovaya

Scaredy Bat
AND THE SUNSCREEN SNATCHER

1. Something Squishy 103
2. The Mix Up 111
3. Suspect Number One 119
4. Saved by Science 125
5. Polka Dot Potato 132
6. This Stinks 142
7. Upside Down 151
8. The Formula 160
9. A Dead End 167
10. A Piggy's Tail 173
11. The Garlic Festival 178
12. We Need a Plan 185
13. Lollipop Surprise 190

Batty Bonuses

Are You Afraid of Clowns? 198
Suspect List 200
Who Did It? 205
Hidden Observation Details Sheet 206
Discussion Questions 211

Can you solve the mystery?

All you need is an eye for detail, a sharp memory, and good logical skills. Join Ellie on her mystery-solving adventure by making a suspect list and figuring out who committed the crime! To help with your sleuthing, you'll find a suspect list template and hidden details observation sheets at the back of the book.

There's a place not far from here
With strange things 'round each corner
It's a town where vampires walk the streets
And unlikely friendships bloom

When there's a mystery to solve
Ellie Spark is the vampire to call
Unless she's scared away like a cat
Poof! There goes that Scaredy Bat

Villains and pesky sisters beware
No spider, clown, or loud noise
Will stop Ellie and her team
From solving crime, one fear at a time

Chapter One
Something Squishy

Ellie fought to catch her breath as she raced down the black-and-white tiled hall, frantically searching for room 302. She couldn't believe that she had slept in, especially on the first day of school.

CRASH!

Her pink backpack slammed to the ground with her not too far behind.

"I am so sorry!" said a high-pitched voice. "Here."

Ellie looked up at the blurry silhouette with which she had collided. She squinted to try to see who it was, but all she could make out was a flurry of long black ringlets and an extended hand with red nails. "Thank you,"

Ellie mumbled as she was helped to her feet.

"And you might need these," added the girl, holding out Ellie's glasses and backpack.

Ellie put her round glasses firmly back on the bridge of her nose and smoothed down her long, brown hair before grabbing her backpack. The girl she had run into not only had

a ton of black hair but also a thick dusting of freckles covering her cheeks and the bluest eyes Ellie had ever seen.

"I'm Ava. I'm new here, and I am completely lost. I'm really sorry again for crashing into you... I was just trying to find my homeroom."

Feeling less disoriented, Ellie gave the girl a big, fanged smile. "It's okay! I know how easy it is to get lost here. It's a pretty big place. What room are you looking for?"

Ava pulled out a yellow, crumpled sheet from her skirt pocket. "Umm, 302."

"Me too!" Ellie exclaimed. "Come on, I think it's just down here."

Ava followed Ellie around the corner, and sure enough, there stood the wooden door with "302" displayed in large, silver letters.

"I guess it was closer than I thought," said Ava. "What's your name?"

"Ellie!"

Ava smiled. "Well, Ellie, I really like your necklace." She pointed to the silver chain with the purple dragon pendant that hung around Ellie's neck. "Where did you get it?"

"It's actually--"

RING! The bell interrupted before Ellie could answer.

"We better go," Ellie said. "I hear that Mr. Bramble loves giving detention when you're late to his class."

"Oh, okay. Well, thanks for the help!" said Ava before rushing into the classroom.

Ellie found the desk with her name messily written with thick, black marker on a tented card, and she was excited to discover that she had been seated beside her best friend, Jessica. Jessica was doodling some fashion sketches in her black notebook. Her red curls bounced around slightly as she tilted her head from side to side to examine her latest creation. Finally, after a satisfied nod, she looked over at Ellie.

"I thought you got lost and were never coming," Jessica joked.

Ellie's breathing and heart rate finally began to slow down. She took in a deep breath before answering. "Well, you aren't wrong about the lost part. But it didn't help that I slept in." She

looked over at her best friend, expecting some sort of crack about her horrible sense of direction, but instead, Jessica was now focused on the other side of the classroom.

"Who is that?" Jessica whispered.

Ellie followed Jessica's stare to Ava, but she was promptly distracted by Fez enthusiastically waving at her. Ellie offered back a wave and a grin as her gaze trailed to a purple stain right below the bat silhouette on Fez's shirt. How that boy always found a way to get food stains on his clothes, she would never understand. Fez made his way across the class.

"Did you hear me?" Jessica asked.

"That's Ava," Ellie finally answered. "We sort of met in the hall earlier."

As Fez took his seat in front of the girls, a horrific garlicky scent filled Ellie's nose. She gagged before covering her nose with her silky shirt collar.

"Fez, why do you smell so much like gross garlic?" Ellie asked.

Fez looked down, sniffed his shirt sleeve, and shrugged. "I've been helping my dad with

his garlic dressing recipe for the Garlic Festival tomorrow."

"Well, you stink!" exclaimed Jessica, followed by a short cough. "I much prefer the blood orange salsa your dad made for the barbecue yesterday."

"It's nothing personal," added Ellie. "Most vampires hate the smell of garlic. But I totally loved your dad's red beans and rice!"

Fez smiled. "Yeah, he went all out for the end-of-summer barbecue." He uncrumpled a piece of paper from his pant pocket and smoothed it out on Ellie's desk. "Are you guys going to the Garlic Festival? We can get you nose plugs!"

Ellie opened her mouth to answer, but her heart jumped to her throat at the sight of a frizzy rainbow afro, a red nose, and a snowy-white face on the cover of the flyer. "Fez! Get that creepy clown away from me!" she shrieked.

Fez picked up the flyer, and his eyebrows slammed together in confusion. "He's not scary; look at that friendly smile." He turned

the flyer back around and held it up in front of Ellie's face.

She shut her eyes as tight as she could. "No! All clowns are terrifying. I. Hate. Clowns."

Fez looked at Jessica, who nodded. "It's true. She won't go near the circus when it comes to town. Not even for their blood pudding."

Fez recrumpled the flyer and stuck it back in his pocket as Jessica let out a short cough and cleared her throat.

"It's safe now," said Jessica. "Well, from the clown. Not the garlic smell."

Ellie slowly opened one eye and then the other, letting out a sigh of relief now that the clown was nowhere in sight.

"Clowns and garlic are both great! I think you guys are just being drama queens," said Fez.

"Agree to disagree." Ellie waved her left hand in front of her nose, trying to fan the garlic smell away while she used her right hand to dig in her pink backpack. "Now where did I put my lavender-scented Monster Spray...? That should help cover up the garlic."

Ellie's hand clutched something squishy and fuzzy that she didn't recognize. She pulled the mystery object out of the backpack and promptly dropped it, jumping out of her chair.

"EEK!" Ellie let out a startled shriek before turning into a bat.

POOF!

Chapter Two
The Mix Up

Ellie fluttered to the top of a wooden bookshelf and silently shook.

"Ms. Spark!" boomed Mr. Bramble from the front of the room. "If you are done with the theatrics, can we start class now?"

POOF! "No! Why are there clowns everywhere?" she squealed as she snapped back into her vampire form. "There's a giant clown head in my bag!"

Gasps and whispers flooded the classroom. Jessica reached down and lifted a squished clown's face off the floor.

"See!" said Ellie, still shaking and sitting on top of the bookshelf.

A laugh exploded over the chatter. "That's

not a clown head, it's just a silly mask." The entire class broke out into giggles, and Ellie's face grew hot with embarrassment. Her attention darted to the boy responsible for the statement. He sat in the back of the classroom with his feet resting on his desk,

his curly black hair parted to the side, and a smug smile pasted on his face. "You're such a scaredy bat," he said.

Ellie had never seen this boy before, yet even he knew her nickname. "I am not!" she snarled. "Someone must have put that mask in there to scare me! And it looked a lot bigger and scarier when I was a small bat."

"Yeah, a *scaredy* bat!" the boy added.

Laughter filled the classroom, and Ellie looked down at his name card. *Jack Grinko.*

"That is enough!" snapped Mr. Bramble. "Miss Spark, take your seat." Ellie hopped down from the bookshelf and sat back at her desk, but not before sticking her tongue out at the mean mystery boy in the back. She didn't know who he was, but she didn't like him.

A hand slowly raised in the air on the opposite side of the class.

"Umm, excuse me, Mr. Bramble…" said a small voice. The whole class's attention turned to Ava. She pointed to her pink backpack. "I think me and Ellie got our backpacks mixed up."

Ellie looked down at the backpack next to her desk, noticing an unfamiliar lion emblem stitched onto the strap. "Oh."

Mr. Bramble ran a hand through his dark hair. "Alright, hurry up and switch back then."

"Sorry," Ava whispered as she rushed toward Ellie's desk. The two girls swapped backpacks, and Ava quickly returned to her seat.

Mr. Bramble gave them an outline of their year and started talking about their upcoming field trip to Jellyfish Lake the following week. "This is going to be an overnight trip," explained Mr. Bramble, "so I will need your permission slips as soon as possible. I should also mention that you will be allowed to choose your own bunk mate." This news sent the class into a flurry of whispers and excitement. Jessica gave Ellie a knowing look, and Ellie nodded back.

"Quiet down! I'm not finished," said Mr. Bramble. "Whomever you choose will also be your partner for a project related to Jellyfish

Lake. This can be a story, a presentation about the landmarks, or a paper on the area's history. You will have a lot of creative freedom for this project, but keep in mind that it will be worth thirty percent of your grade, so choose your partner wisely. I'm going to pass around the permission slips, so take a few minutes to pair up. If you can't find a partner, I can find someone for you."

Jessica gave Ellie a big smile that showed off her perfectly white fangs. "I am so excited!" she exclaimed. "My mom told me that a lot of celebrities like to vacation at Jellyfish Lake, so maybe we'll see one. I heard that last year that blond guy from the movie *Werewolf Island* vacationed there but forgot his sunscreen, so he ended up with permanent blue spots. It totally ended his acting career."

Ellie's mouth dropped open. "That's horrible! Do you know if it drained his transformational powers too?"

Fez turned around and leaned into the conversation. "Umm, why would a sunburn

leave blue spots? Or drain transformational powers?"

"That's just what happens," Ellie explained. "Vampires burn really easily in the sun, and if we do, we can be stuck with permanent blue spots. The sun can even drain our abilities. I mean, since I can't always control turning into a bat, I sometimes wonder if that would be such a bad thing…"

"Woah, I had no idea!" exclaimed Fez. "When I get a sunburn, my skin just turns red and peels."

"If you don't have enough sunscreen, make sure to get your parents to order more tonight," said Jessica.

Ellie smiled. "Don't worry. I just got a new bottle yesterday. It's right here." She began digging through her backpack, and slowly her smile disappeared. "Where is it?" She dumped the entire contents onto her desk, but there was no sunscreen.

"Did you forget it at home?" asked Jessica.

"No," said Ellie. "It's a brand-new bottle! If I don't find it, I am so dead."

Fez shrugged. "What's the big deal? Can't you just go to the store and buy a new one? I have a few bucks I can lend you." Fez pulled a few bills from his pocket.

"No, it's not like human sunscreen, Fez. Every vampire needs a special formula made because there are so many different skin types. That makes it super expensive."

Fez pulled a few more bills from his pocket.

"Like a hundred dollars expensive."

"Oh." Fez put his money away. "I can't help you there."

"I'm sure you'll find it," assured Jessica with a meek smile.

The lump in Ellie's throat grew larger, and her palms began to sweat. She hoped Jessica was right, because otherwise, Ellie was in serious trouble. She needed that sunscreen.

Chapter Three
Suspect Number One

"Maybe Ava has it!" Ellie looked across the room at Ava, who was talking and laughing with a short blond girl. Ellie sprang from her chair, raced across the room, and tapped Ava on the shoulder. "Do you have my sunscreen?" she asked in a quick huff, making her question sound like one long word.

"Umm, your sunscreen? I don't think so, sorry."

"You sure you didn't accidentally take it out of my backpack thinking it was yours?"

Ava shook her head. "Mine is in a special bottle, because I kept losing it and my parents were tired of paying for extra. See!" She unzipped the front pouch of her backpack and

pulled out a clear purple bottle attached to the bag with a gold chain and decorated with red gems.

Ellie's eyes lit up. "Wow, that is so pretty! Mine is just in a plain white bottle. You know, the usual one with the funny-looking sun on the front."

Ava nodded. "Yup! My brother uses that one." She pointed to Jack, the boy who had made fun of Ellie earlier. Ellie looked at Jack, who was twirling a string of pink gum hanging from his mouth around his finger. How could someone so mean be related to someone as sweet as Ava? Then again, you couldn't pick your siblings. Thoughts of Ellie's little sister, Penny, flooded her mind but were quickly pushed away with the sound of Ava's voice.

"Sorry again about the backpack mix-up," said Ava. "And sorry if my clown mask scared you. I wanted to say something sooner..." She lowered her voice to a whisper. "But Mr. Bramble kind of terrifies me."

Ellie smiled. "Don't worry, I think he scares

everyone." Both girls directed their attention toward the teacher writing down instructions on the large blackboard and shared a small laugh.

"Why do you have a clown mask?" Ellie asked.

"I'm volunteering at the Garlic Festival!" Ava said enthusiastically.

"Oh, well, have fun," said Ellie, not entirely sure why anyone would volunteer to be a creepy clown.

When Ellie got back to her seat, she beamed at a short boy with brown curly hair and glasses sitting beside her.

"Hey, Tink! Why are you so late?" she asked.

Tink adjusted the glasses on the bridge of his nose and groaned. "My alarm didn't go off and now I have detention. Detention on the first day of school. Can you believe it?" He sighed as he showed Ellie the pink detention slip.

"If it makes you feel better, I'm having a terrible day too. I was almost late, I accidentally turned into a bat, and I lost my sunscreen. I thought the new girl Ava had it, but nope."

"Sunscreen? Oh right, I've read about the blue dots thing." Tink paused for a moment in thought. "So, do you think you lost it or someone stole it? Kind of sounds like a mystery."

Ellie's eyes widened with excitement. It did sound like a mystery. This could be a chance for Ellie to put her detective skills to the test.

Mr. Bramble instructed everyone to go back

to their desks, and he started to explain more about the school year, but Ellie wasn't paying attention. She opened her small, purple notepad with the silver skeleton key on the front and wrote down something she learned from her favorite mystery series, *The Amazing Vampire Detective.*

Suspects must have two things: Access & Motive

She tapped her pencil lightly on the page as she thought about who could have taken her sunscreen. She had already ruled out Ava, so who else, and why?

1. *Pesky Penny – always stealing my stuff*
2. *Aliens – might need sunscreen when flying close to sun*
3. *Jack Grinko – seems like a bully*

Her sister Penny loved stealing Ellie's stuff, plus she was in some sort of weird "potion-making" phase where she snatched Ellie's lotions and hair products to pretend she was a witch creating magical brews. She was suspect number one, and Ellie was going to investigate her when she got home… But there was one small problem. Ellie looked out the window at the sun starting to peek out from behind the rain clouds.

Without her sunscreen, how was she ever going to get home?

Chapter Four
Saved by Science

Ring! The final bell of the day blasted through the hall, and Ellie emptied her backpack for the hundredth time—her sunscreen was still nowhere to be found.

She marched up to Jessica's locker and found her friend carefully applying pink lip gloss and looking into her small black locker mirror.

"Jess, I need to borrow your sunscreen."

"Sorry, I don't wear any," said Jessica with a shrug as she wiped a bit of gloss off with her finger.

Ellie's mouth gaped. "How!? You would have tons of blue dots if you didn't wear some."

Jessica closed her locker and shook her head. "Nope, not with the shot they came out with

last year. I get it once a month and I'm good to go! But hey, even if I did have sunscreen, you know it wouldn't work for your skin type."

Ellie groaned. "I wish I could get that shot, but my dad doesn't think it's as good as the sunscreen. He said he had a patient that had the shot but still ended up with permanent blue spots."

Jessica snickered. "Ellie, even if you were allowed to get the shot, you're terrified of needles." Ellie's face turned white at the thought. Jessica was right. "Anyway, I have to go meet my mom on the set of the new movie they're shooting in town, *Vampires in Paradise.* I'll see you tomorrow!"

Ellie waved at her friend and then dug in her backpack for something to protect her from the sun so she could get home. Nothing. She didn't need her sunscreen this morning because it was cloudy and raining, but now the sun was full blast. Continuing her search, she rounded the corner to the gym, and a sour smell hit her nose, while an odd sight caught her eye—a scrawny man with frizzy black hair

that everyone referred to as "Stinky Lou" was digging in a large garbage bin. No, he wasn't called Stinky Lou because he dug in the garbage. It wasn't what he usually did… or at least Ellie didn't think so. The truth was that Stinky Lou was a rare sight around town, and no one quite knew why he stank, but there were a couple of theories.

The simple one was that he never showered. But whenever Ellie saw him, he never looked

dirty—he just smelled awful. Another popular explanation was that he rubbed himself with garlic, wet dog fur, old socks, and rotten fruit so kids would leave him alone. And finally, there was a legend that the ghosts in his house put a curse on him that made him permanently stink. That was always the one Ellie chose to believe, even though deep down she knew it was kind of ridiculous. She gulped, quietly turned around, and headed back down the hall.

Ellie went to the science lab next and started rummaging through drawers and cabinets. She found beakers, funnels, and magnets, but nothing that would protect her from the sun. After what felt like her twentieth drawer, Tink walked into the classroom.

"Hey, Tink, aren't you supposed to be in detention?" asked Ellie.

Tink turned around. "Oh, hi, Ellie. Yeah, but after-school detention doesn't start until next week. What are you doing here?"

Ellie bit her bottom lip as she looked around the room. "I need to get home. I don't have my sunscreen, so I need something to cover

me and protect me from the sun."

Tink thought for a moment. "I have just the thing." He headed to a drawer at the front of the class and pulled out a large roll of tin foil. "It won't protect you from the heat, but it should save you from the sun."

"Done!" Ellie exclaimed. She held out her arms as Tink wrapped the tin foil around her body.

Crinkle! Crinkle!

"You sure found this quickly," Ellie said over the sound of the foil. "I had science in here last year, and I still don't remember where the goggles go."

Tink let out a small laugh. "Well, I guess I spend a lot of time here." His lips made a tight, straight line. Tink paused, and the crinkling of the foil followed. "When my foster mom gets busy with her wedding planning, I come here a lot just to fiddle around. It beats being bored at home… plus it can be lonely there sometimes."

"Oh, maybe you just need your own science lab at home," Ellie said, trying to lighten the mood a bit.

Tink's slight smile reappeared. "Oh, I wish! That's the dream."

Ellie smiled back. "Well, you can come to my house for dinner if you want."

"What are you having?"

"I think my Mom said that blood pudding was today's after-school snack, and liver, rare steak, and boiled beets were supper." Her mouth started to water just talking about it.

Tink's face turned green. "I think I am going to pass, but thanks anyway."

"Okay, but you're missing out!" Once her entire body was covered in multiple layers and the only parts of her showing were her eyes and mouth, she shifted her stiff body around.

"You sure about dinner?" she asked one last time.

"One hundred percent," said Tink. "But thanks anyway."

"Okay, well, thanks for your help!" With her shiny silver shell, she looked like she was wearing a bad Halloween costume. She crinkled her way out the door and began her run home.

Chapter Five
Polka Dot Potato

Crinkle! Crinkle!

Ellie ran through her front door, drenched in sweat, and leaned forward to catch her breath. She made it home, but she had never been so hot in her life. She raced to the kitchen trash can to begin peeling off the layers of shiny foil and found her pesky sister, Penny, sitting at the nearby table in the corner.

With her face full of pudding, Penny looked up at Ellie, who was now frantically trying to free herself from her silver shell. "You look like a baked potato!" Penny declared, shrieking with laughter.

Ellie paused her peeling efforts to shoot Penny a dirty look. "Yeah, well, at least I know

how to put food in my mouth and not all over my face."

Penny's smile quickly turned to a pout. "Mom! Ellie is being mean."

"Shhh!" Ellie urged. "Don't call Mom."

"Why not?" Penny crossed her arms.

"Because I said so."

Not pleased with that answer, Penny tried again. "Mom! Mom! MO--"

Ellie bolted to the table and covered her sister's mouth with her tinfoil-covered hand. "If you stop, I'll give you whatever you want."

Penny nodded in agreement after a couple seconds of thought, and Ellie slowly removed her hand.

"Why? You don't want Mom to know you're a big baked potato? Why *are* you a baked potato?"

"No more questions. What do you want me to give you?" asked Ellie.

Penny looked down at the full bowl of blood pudding set out at Ellie's spot and then back at her own, almost-empty bowl. "I want your blood pudding!"

"Fine."

"For the next month," Penny added.

Ellie's jaw dropped. "No way! I am not giving you my favorite food in the world for a whole month!"

Penny smirked. "Fine, then I'm telling. Mom! MO--"

"Argh! Two weeks, that's it!" Ellie shoved the bowl toward her sister, and it slid across the table. She couldn't risk her parents finding out that she had lost her sunscreen, especially since it was a new bottle. They could only afford one bottle per month because it was so expensive, and Ellie had just gotten her new one. Penny started shoveling the second bowl of pudding into her mouth.

"Did you take my sunscreen?" Ellie narrowed her eyes at her sister.

"Nope." Penny sputtered pudding across the table with her answer, and Ellie watched for her sister's signature lip twitch. Penny was a horrible liar whose lip always twitched when she was trying to hide the truth, but it was hard to see under the mess of pudding. Penny looked at Ellie and started laughing.

"What's so funny?" Ellie asked.

A dribble of pudding fell from Penny's mouth. "You also have polka dots. You're now the funniest potato ever!"

Ellie's eyes widened. "No!" She stumbled up the stairs to look in the bathroom mirror and found subtle green splotches sprinkled across her face. A wave of relief washed over her. Green meant that they would fade; it was only the blue ones that were permanent. Clearly, tinfoil wasn't enough protection, though. She had to find her sunscreen ASAP, and she knew exactly where to start looking.

Penny was her prime suspect. Her sister was always "borrowing" her stuff, so why should this be any different? Ellie pushed open her sister's door to find toys blanketing the floor. She didn't know how Penny ever found anything in this mess, and she certainly didn't know how she was going to find her sunscreen.

After rummaging through the toybox, under the bed, and in the closet, Ellie found a white plastic bottle hiding under a jean jacket. "Aha!" She looked at the yellow label, and her

heart raced with excitement as she recognized the quirky little sun logo with the straw hat and red sunglasses. This was definitely the specially formulated sunscreen, but was it hers? She flipped over the bottle, only to have the words "Made for Penny Spark" instantly crush her hope. She threw the bottle onto the pink coffin bed and grabbed the purple scarf that

she thought she had lost before heading to her own bedroom. No sooner did she enter her room than she heard her name.

"Ellie, dinner!" called Mom from downstairs. Ellie's stomach vibrated as it growled like a lion. She checked her mirror. The green splotches had faded but were definitely still there. Not wanting to answer sunscreen questions, she had to think of how to cover them.

"Ellie!"

And fast. "Coming!" Ellie called back. She spun in place a few times as she looked around for a possible solution. She wasn't allowed to wear makeup, and hoods only covered her hair. What was she going to do? Suddenly, the dark purple scarf in her hand caught her eye. *It might just work,* she thought. She wrapped it around her face a few times so only her eyes and mouth poked out. And when she looked in the mirror, she couldn't help but think she looked like a fashionable mummy.

"Ellie! It's getting cold," called Mom.

"Coming!" Ellie called back once again. The purple scarf would have to do.

She made her way downstairs, and a mixture of salty and sweet aromas wafted through the kitchen. Ellie casually sat down at the table, and all eyes fell on her as she looked down at her plate filled with liver, rare steak, and a seared cow's heart. "Wow, this looks really good!" she said.

Ellie's mom looked over at her husband. "Do you want to ask, or should I?"

Ellie's dad shook his head. "This is all yours." He returned to his plateful of vegetables.

"Why are you wrapped in a scarf?" Mom asked.

Ellie stuffed some liver into her mouth to buy herself more time to answer, but Penny was more prompt.

"I think she just likes dressing up. Earlier today she was a big baked potato!" Penny exclaimed. Ellie kicked Penny's leg under the table. "Ow!" Penny cried.

"What is going on?" asked Mom, crossing her arms over her chest.

Ellie swallowed her food. "Oh, um. I'm writing a paper on mummies and wanted to know what it feels like to be one. Don't you like it?"

Dad smiled. "That's my girl! Glad you're taking school so seriously."

Mom sighed. "Well, purple has always looked good on you. Must you wear your scarf at the table, though?"

"Yeah, must you wear *my* scarf at the table?" Penny echoed.

"This is my scarf!" Ellie sneered.

"Are you sure about that, polka dot potato?" Not wanting to risk a lecture on responsibility and sunscreen, Ellie gritted her teeth.

"I'll give it back to you when I'm done."

Satisfied with that answer, Penny happily went back to stuffing her face.

After getting through dinner with no more questions, Ellie headed back to her bedroom. She took a seat on her coffin bed beside the wall covered floor-to-ceiling with posters from detective movies and shows, mostly with her favorite detective, Hailey Haddie. She looked at the newspaper clipping with her, Tink, Jessica, and Fez smiling below the headline, "The Small Detective Team That Saved The Royal Vampire Wedding." Ellie smiled at the memory before focusing on a photo of Hailey Haddie. In the photo, Hailey was chewing a pen cap as she made a list of suspects. Ellie decided it was time to further examine hers.

1. *Pesky Penny – always stealing my stuff*
2. *Aliens – might need sunscreen when flying close to sun*
3. *Jack Grinko – seems like a bully*

Satisfied with her possibilities, she gave a nod as she read them over. But after thinking a bit more, she grabbed her pen and made a few changes.

1. ~~*Pesky Penny*~~ *(No sign of my sunscreen in her room)*
2. ~~*Aliens*~~ *(They fly so close to the sun they would need much stronger sunscreen)*
3. *Jack Grinko – seems like a bully*

She narrowed down to one suspect, Jack Grinko. He liked to be a bully, and this would be a great way to do it.

Jack was now her prime suspect.

Chapter Six
This Stinks

The next day, Ellie traded her tinfoil protection for her favorite turquoise trench coat, detective hat, wool mittens, the purple scarf, pants, and sunglasses. She loved the detective hat and coat together; however, the rest was way too hot and made the outfit clash. But she didn't care. She wasn't taking any chances.

As soon as she got to school, she ran into the brick building and threw off her itchy mittens and damp scarf. Losing her sunscreen in the winter would have been much easier, and a whole lot less sweaty. She made her way to the science lab to replace the tinfoil she'd borrowed and found Tink in the same spot she'd left him.

"Did you sleep here?" she joked.

Tink laughed. "No, when the janitor leaves, I have to, too. But I do have something for you!" He handed Ellie a small bottle. "I found this sunscreen recipe on the internet, and the reviews say it works great, but only for about twenty minutes."

Ellie broke into a big, fangy smile. "Thank you so much, Tink! This is so nice of you." She lunged toward her friend and wrapped her arms around him.

"You're welcome," Tink replied.

Ellie broke away from the hug and smoothed out her trench coat. "Hey, have you seen Fez and Jessica anywhere today? I want to talk to you guys about a sunscreen snatcher lead."

"Sunscreen snatcher?" asked Tink. Just as Ellie pulled out her notebook with the suspect list, a wave of noise washed in from outside. Ellie and Tink raced over to the window to see what all the fuss was about. Right in the middle of a group stood Fez and the mean kid from homeroom, Jack Grinko. Standing almost a foot taller than stout Fez, Jack towered over the boy. This made it easy to keep the mystery object he held just out of Fez's reach.

Jack dangled the white object, and Ellie's eyes bulged. "That's my sunscreen!" she exclaimed. But when she turned to look at Tink, he was nowhere in sight. Ellie snatched up the homemade sunscreen and began lathering herself with the thick lotion that smelled faintly of black licorice. Ellie gagged slightly.

She hated black licorice. She held her breath as she finished applying and raced outside.

She made her way to the scene to find Tink with his hands on his hips, standing beside Fez. With Tink being even shorter than Fez, freakishly tall and lanky Jack now looked like a giant.

"G- give it back!" Tink demanded in a shaky voice.

Jack laughed. "What if I don't? What's a little nerd like you going to do about it?"

Tink lowered his hands from his hips and sucked in a deep breath that puffed out his chest. "I'm going to… I'm going to…" He paused to think for a second. "I'm going to turn you blue!" He let out his breath in one big huff.

"Blue!?" Jack laughed. "How are you going to do that?"

Tink mumbled a few unclear words and looked down at the ground.

Jack's laughter was overpowered by the first bell. He walked over to Tink and looked him straight in the eye. "You're lucky you were saved by the bell, dweebs." Jack shoved the bottle into Fez's hands and took off.

Ellie rushed over to Fez and Tink. "Are you guys okay?"

"Yeah, are you okay?" echoed a soft voice behind Ellie.

Ellie turned. Ava was walking toward them. Tink and Fez nodded in unison. "I was just minding my own business when Jack decided to steal this," Fez said, showing off the white bottle.

"Wow," said Ava. "Jack can be such a jerk!"

Everyone agreed.

"I hardly know him, and I already don't like him," said Ellie.

"Same here," said Tink.

"Me too," agreed Fez.

Ava sighed. "Yup, he has that effect on people. Well, I should get to class. Glad you're okay!" And with that Ava gave a quick wave before rushing inside.

Fez's eyes were glued to Ava as she pranced off, and the white bottle slipped from his hand, crashing to the pebbly, gray gravel. "Oops."

"What is that, anyway?" asked Tink, looking at the bottle. Fez bent down and picked it up.

"My sunscreen!" cried Ellie, excitedly snatching the bottle from Fez's hand as he straightened.

A frown appeared on Fez's face. "I wish people would stop taking my garlic dressing like that! That's exactly what Jack did."

"Garlic dressing?" said both Tink and Ellie. Ellie read the label on the bottle: "Fitzgerald's Garlic Dressing – Entry #21." She flipped the bottle over to reveal a yellow garlic head wearing red sunglasses and a big smile.

"Oh." The corners of Ellie's mouth turned down. "It looked exactly like my sunscreen bottle. What is this?"

Fez beamed proudly. "My dad's entry to the dressing competition at the Garlic Festival! The garlic mixture still needed to cool before being added to the plain dressing base, so I agreed to bottle it and submit it to the festival after school. Doesn't it smell great?" Fez twisted the cap off the bottle, and the scent of garlic flooded the air.

"No, that's horrible!" Ellie shrieked.

"I think it smells delicious," Tink said, leaning closer. "Do I also smell paprika?"

"Yeah." Fez nodded enthusiastically. "I can't wait to snack on the extra bottle my dad left out for me."

Jessica walked up to the group wearing a leopard-print sweater and a big smile. "Hey, guys, didn't the first bell already ring— Oh. My. Gosh! What is that awful smell?" Jessica pinched her nose shut and backed away.

Ellie laughed. "See!" She pulled out her notepad from her pocket. "Okay, guys, my sunscreen is still missing. I wanted to talk to you about Jack as a suspect, but now I'm not so sure. I think he would have rubbed it in my face by now, but he could have made the switch when Ava and I collided in the hall. They *are* siblings, so maybe they're working together. What do you think?"

"I don't think so," Jessica answered in a nasally voice. "I was in class pretty early, and Jack was there the whole time."

"Oh." Ellie's shoulders slumped. "If Jack has an alibi, then I don't have any more suspects. Now I'm never going to find my sunscreen, and my parents are going to ground me forever."

Fez patted Ellie on the shoulder. "Now *this* stinks."

With her nose still pinched, Jessica continued to talk in a nasally voice. "Don't give up yet, Ellie! Speaking of things that stink, I saw Stinky Lou digging in the school garbage yesterday, and he's been spotted around town

pulling bottles of sunscreen from bins. Maybe he could be behind it?"

Ellie did an excited little hop. "Yes, I saw him randomly digging in the school garbage yesterday, too. Super suspicious. Do you really think he stole my sunscreen, though?"

"Well, he hardly ever leaves his house, so maybe he needs sunscreen to go outside more or something," Jessica said. The group nodded in agreement. It was possible.

"Let's check it out after school!" Ellie decided.

Satisfied with the new lead, Ellie updated her list.

1. ~~Pesky Penny~~ *(No sign of my sunscreen in her bedroom)*
2. ~~Aliens~~ *(They fly so close to the sun they would need much stronger sunscreen)*
3. ~~Jack Grinko~~ *(Just a big jerk, not a sunscreen snatcher)*
4. Stinky Lou – seen taking sunscreen from trash & might need it to go outside more

Chapter Seven
Upside Down

Jessica, Tink, and Ellie stood on the concrete steps of the old house on the corner of 4th Street. Fez went to drop off the garlic dressing at the festival, but he promised to join the group later.

When Ellie was younger, she would always hold her breath going by this house, because other kids said that ghosts lived there and you might inhale them. Being this close to the house, she suddenly believed it was haunted more than ever. If only she could hold her breath for more than a few seconds…

"You know what? My sunscreen isn't that important," Ellie said matter-of-factly. "Tink made me this weird licorice stuff that lets me

go outside for a bit. Let's go grab a bite to eat, I'm starving!"

Just as Ellie began to turn on her heel, Jessica grabbed her arm. "No, you need your sunscreen."

Ellie waved her off. "Nah. I can wait a few weeks for the new stuff."

Tink silently followed the conversation, shifting uncomfortably from one foot to the next. He had spent enough time with Jessica and Ellie to know not to get in the middle of their bickering.

"No, no, you cannot," Jessica said. "That trip to Jellyfish Lake is in one week, and you won't have your new sunscreen by then."

Ellie's face turned blank. She hadn't thought of that before.

"Do you really want to stay at school instead of going on the big trip?"

"Maybe it wouldn't be so bad…" Ellie started.

"Fine. Maybe I'll ask that new girl, Ava, to be my roommate."

Ellie's mouth gaped. "But I was going to be your roommate!"

"And I also learned recently that Jellyfish Lake is one of Hailey Haddie's favorite spots. So, who knows, she might be there."

Hailey Haddie was one of Ellie's all-time heroes, and Ellie didn't know what she would do if she missed the opportunity to meet her.

Tink finally decided to throw in a word. "It would be easier to have a partner that has actually experienced the trip, since we have to do an assignment on it after. And it would be a bummer to miss out on Hailey Haddie."

Ellie shot an unimpressed look at him, and Tink's gaze trailed away from her. "Just saying," he added.

"Fine!" Ellie exclaimed. "We're going to do this!" She marched up to the door and banged the metal knocker against the cracking wood. After her knocks were only answered with silence, she tried again. Over a minute passed, but there was still no answer.

"Maybe we should try again later," Tink offered. Just then, an orange cat raced up to the door and gave it a slight push. The big door slowly creaked open. Clearly pleased with his

actions, the kitty's tail waved from side to side in the air, and she slunk in.

"Hello? Hello!?" Jessica called through the front entrance. "Is anyone home?" The sound of her voice echoed back at her, but no one else answered.

"Maybe we should just go in," Ellie suggested. "I'm sure if Stinky Lou stole my sunscreen, he wouldn't risk bringing it out in public. Come on!" Before either of her friends could object or she could change her mind, Ellie entered the creepy house.

"Ellie. Ellie!" Tink and Jessica called after her in loud whispers, but she had already disappeared around the corner.

Ellie found herself in a large hallway filled with the smell of pinewood and lined with portraits of cats. Some were photos printed on canvas, while others were large oil paintings of cats in various costumes. There was even one particularly large artwork of a plump orange cat dressed as a clown. A large shiver made its way up Ellie's spine, and her arms broke out in goosebumps. There was something so

creepy about clowns—especially cat clowns, apparently.

"Ellie!" came a loud whisper. Ellie jumped slightly and whipped her head around. Jessica and Tink had joined her inside the house. She waved before giving the cat portraits one last look.

Jessica came up beside her. "Wow, these are..." Jessica trailed off, not knowing how to finish her sentence.

"Kinda cool," offered Tink with a satisfied nod.

Jessica's jaw dropped. "Not the words I was going for."

"I really like this one." Tink pointed to a cat in a lab coat wearing goggles with beakers all around him.

"You would," said Jessica with an eye roll.

"Guys, we need to look for clues," Ellie interrupted. "Let's try the kitchen."

The trio found the kitchen through the living room. It was a lot less dusty than the rest of the house, and an assortment of lab equipment littered the center island. There were vials of

chemicals, beakers, a Bunsen burner, and tons of notes scattered everywhere.

"Maybe that scientist cat in the picture lives here," Jessica joked. But Ellie was already looking for clues, and Tink was too busy examining all the science stuff to hear her. Jessica joined the search with a sigh. "What exactly are we looking for?" she asked.

"A bottle of sunscreen with my name on it… or clues to help us find it," Ellie answered.

Jessica nodded and began lifting a stack of papers off the counter.

"Don't touch those!" Tink hissed. "They're probably in a very specific order. You have to be super careful around science experiments or you could ruin the whole thing."

Jessica dropped the papers in surrender and moved her search to another area of the kitchen. Ellie began opening the cupboards, which were mainly filled with glass containers and the occasional pot and pan. But then she opened a big drawer labeled "SUN."

"Look!" Ellie cried.

"Shhh!" hushed Jessica.

Ellie tried again in a whisper. "Look." She pointed at the drawer. There were over eighty white bottles neatly lined up in rows, all labeled with black marker.

"One might be yours," said Jessica before both girls started sifting through the collection.

CRASH! POOF!

The piercing sound of shattering glass made Jessica jump and instantly caused Ellie to turn into a bat.

"Sorry, that was just me," said Tink.

Jessica put her hands firmly on her hips. "Whatever happened to 'being super careful around science experiments,'" she said in a mocking voice.

BANG!

Suddenly the pantry whipped open to reveal a man hanging upside down by his feet, and he was staring directly at Tink and Jessica.

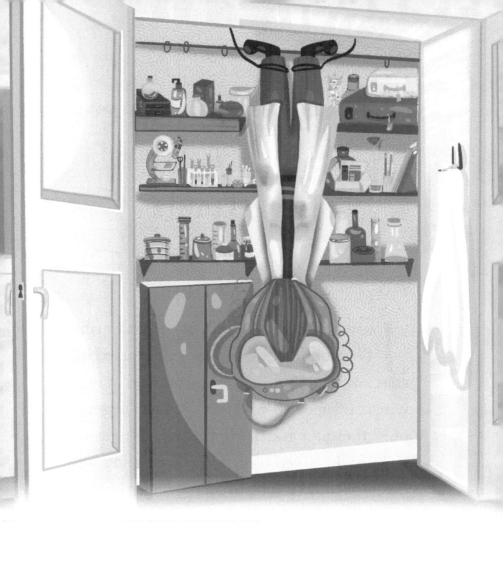

Chapter Eight
The Formula

Jessica shrieked and ran into Tink's arms. The upside-down man wore a stained lab coat and had some sort of metal helmet with wires strapped to his head. "What is going on?" the man asked. He flipped himself upright and walked over to the trembling duo before silently turning his attention to the shattered glass on the floor.

"You know, you really *do* need to be more careful around science equipment," he scolded before grabbing a nearby broom.

"We-we should go," Tink said, grabbing Jessica's hand.

"Not yet," said the man. "You break it, you clean it." He extended the broom toward Tink.

Tink shakily let go of Jessica's hand to grab the broom and began sweeping the mess.

"You're kinda sweaty," said Jessica, wiping her newly-released hand on her dress.

"Yeah, well, I nearly had a heart attack just now, so it makes sense," Tink muttered.

"Sorry if I scared you," said the man as he let out a breath before taking off his strange helmet device and sitting on a charred stool. "But what are you two doing in my house? Don't you know that you're trespassing?"

Tink nodded. "Yes, sir. We are very, very sorry."

"We were just looking for our friend Ellie's sunscreen," Jessica replied.

"Well, I hardly feel that is an excuse to break into my house. And shouldn't she be looking for her own sunscreen?"

Tink paused his sweeping efforts for a moment, and he and Jessica exchanged a look. "Well, she is…" said Jessica. *POOF!* Ellie appeared in the middle of the kitchen, causing the man to almost fall off his stool.

Ellie's cheeks flushed as she gave a small

wave and mumbled a soft, "Sorry." Strangely, Lou didn't smell bad today; in fact, he kind of smelled like warm apple cider with a hint of cinnamon.

"You kids are going to be the death of old Stinky Lou," said the man. The gang exchanged another round of looks with each other. "Yes, I know what everyone calls me," Lou said, confirming what they were all thinking.

"Why were you digging through the trash at our school yesterday?" Ellie inquired, placing her hands on her hips.

Lou pointed to his helmet on the counter. "I'm good friends with your science teacher, Mr. Crunkle, and he allows me to take my pick from the recycled electronics bin for my experiments."

Ellie took her hands off her hips, and her shoulders slumped. "So, you didn't steal my sunscreen?"

Lou let out a loud laugh that sounded like a small marble was clanking around in the back of his throat. "Why would I want your sunscreen? I have several dozen bottles over

there." He pointed to the open drawer. "You're welcome to help yourself."

Tink swept the glass into the dustpan and dumped it into the nearby trash before handing the broom back to Lou. "Sorry, again," Tink muttered, barely able to make eye contact.

Lou took the broom. "Well, I suppose no harm done," he replied, offering a small smile that put Tink at ease. Ellie walked over to the drawer and resumed sorting through the contents. All the bottles were plain and white with batch numbers written on them, along with short comments. *Batch #2 (Runny), Batch #8 (Chunky), Batch #5 (Slimy).*

Tink and Lou had begun talking about the helmet that Lou wore earlier, and how Lou believed that it might cure the hiccups. Lou explained that he often got the hiccups that would wake him up when he slept hanging upside down, so he wanted a way to fix that.

Ellie looked over at Tink and Lou discussing science and then back down at the drawer. "I don't think Lou took my sunscreen," she whispered to Jessica. "He seems to have a whole lot of his own. Do you think any of this would work for my skin type?"

Jessica shrugged. "Only one way to find out. Well, two, actually. But we won't go the 'cook you in the sun' route. Hey, Lou!"

Lou paused his conversation and turned to Jessica.

"Which one of these would work for skin type 4B?"

Lou smiled. "Any bottle will work just fine. If you can find anything after batch twelve, though, it has the best consistency."

"What do you mean, 'any bottle will work just fine?' Sunscreens don't work the same for

all vampires, you know," said Tink.

Lou gave a big smile, revealing his slightly off-white fangs. "Oh, I know," he said. "But my formula does."

Chapter Nine
A Dead End

Lou explained that he was trying to create a "one-size-fits-all" vampire sunscreen, and he had succeeded. Well, except for one minor detail.

"This stinks!" Jessica exclaimed, taking a whiff from one of the bottles in the drawer.

Lou laughed. "Yup, I've been trying for years to fix the scent, but I can't seem to change it without interfering with how it works."

Ellie's excitement faded as she took in the sour smell of the sunscreen—she finally understood why Lou always seemed to stink. It also made sense why he had been seen collecting old sunscreen bottles around town.

"Why wouldn't you just get a sunscreen shot or the special sunscreen that doesn't smell?" Ellie asked.

Lou waved his hand dismissively. "Too expensive. Why bother when I have a perfectly good sunscreen that works? The money that I save allows me to buy some science equipment every month, and I would far prefer that over smelling 'nice.' Plus, I am really close to getting the recipe to smell better." Lou pulled a piece of paper with the sunscreen formula across the counter, and Tink readjusted his glasses as he glanced over it.

"This is genius!" Tink exclaimed.

Ellie took a whiff from batch number one and nearly fainted. "I need some fresh air," she said. Jessica was the only one listening, though, as the two boys chatted about the sunscreen formula.

Jessica and Ellie took a seat on the front step, and Ellie ran her hands over her face. "Well, that was a dead-end," she said.

"What was a dead end?" Fez asked as he walked up from the sidewalk and down the overgrown path that led to the porch. "Did you find your sunscreen?"

Ellie shook her head. "Nope. Did you drop off your dad's garlic dressing?"

Fez grinned proudly. "Sure did!" His eyes scanned the porch. "Hey, where's Tink?" Both girls silently pointed inside. Fez's eyes scanned over the old house, with its boarded windows, vines growing up the side, and a roof that looked like it might cave in at any moment.

His smile faded, and he gulped. "Tink is in there? By himself?"

"No," Jessica said matter-of-factly. Fez exhaled in relief. "He's in there with Stinky Lou--I mean, Lou."

"What!?" Fez cried.

"He's really nice," reassured Jessica. "Him and Tink seem to get along well. Turns out Lou loves science, just like Tink."

"Yup," said Ellie. "I'm sure you can go in and see Tink. It isn't so scary on the inside, well, minus the clown cat painting."

"There are cats!" Fez exclaimed, his worry instantly disappearing. He loved animals, especially cats. And dogs. And iguanas. And penguins. Okay, he loved all of them. As if on cue, the orange cat that they had seen earlier appeared in the entrance. "Oh, hi, kitty!" Fez said, perhaps a bit too loudly, as it startled the cat back inside. Seemingly fearless, Fez followed the cat. "Oh no, come back. I just want to pet you," was the last thing Ellie and Jessica heard before Fez disappeared into the house.

Jessica giggled. "He sure does like cats." But

Ellie wasn't listening. She was zoned out, staring at a big oak tree across the street. "We're going to find your sunscreen," Jessica said. She gave her friend a playful jab with her elbow. "Cheer up."

Ellie shook her head. "I think you should just ask Ava to be your partner for Jellyfish

Lake. I'm not going to be able to go." Tears welled up in Ellie's eyes.

"I don't want Ava to be my partner!" Jessica exclaimed. "You're my best friend, and I want you to come with me." A tear slipped down Ellie's cheek, and she quickly wiped it away. "I just said I would ask Ava earlier because I wanted you to find your sunscreen."

A piercing scream suddenly burst from the house.

Chapter Ten
A Piggy's Tail

Jessica and Ellie ran into the house to find everyone in the living room. They watched as two furry ears sprouted from Fez's head and a pink snout formed over his nose.

"What's happening?" said Fez, looking down at his hands turning to hooves.

Tink and Lou stood on the other side of the living room. "Don't panic," Lou commanded. He looked down at the cat brushing up against Fez. "Did you happen to pet Miss Meow Meow Face?"

Ellie couldn't help but snicker slightly. That was the best cat name she had ever heard. Fez nodded rapidly, making his pink ears flop

around. Now Tink started laughing, and Jessica too.

"Guys, this isn't funny," Fez insisted.

A small smile tugged at Lou's face as he calmly tried to explain the situation. "Miss Meow Face may have rolled around in some of my transformation powder this morning.

And while it has no effect on animals, if it was on her fur, it probably transferred to you when you pet her."

Fez scrunched his pink snout. "What did I turn into?" He looked toward the TV and caught his reflection in the darkened glass. "I'm a piglet!" he exclaimed. The whole room tried to stifle their laughter.

"Don't worry, there's an easy fix," Lou explained. "All you need to do is eat some garlic, and voila. Good as new… Unfortunately, I'm all out."

Fez's ears perked up. "I have some in my backpack!" He threw his bag on the ground and began trying to undo the zipper, but his newfound hooves made it nearly impossible.

"Here." Ellie kneeled beside Fez and helped him unzip the front compartment.

"Just grab that bottle in there and open it for me," said Fez. "It's the extra bottle of garlic dressing my dad left for me to snack on."

Ellie quickly reached in and pulled out a pair of turquoise sunglasses with bat wings on each corner.

"Hey, these are my sunglasses!" Ellie exclaimed. "Why do you have them?"

"Oh!" Fez oinked. "Someone left them at my house during the end-of-year barbecue. I meant to ask if they belonged to any of you."

Ellie tucked the glasses in her pocket and reached into the bag again. She pulled out a white bottle and popped the cap. She squeezed a bit on Fez's tongue, and they waited. After swishing the dressing in his mouth a bit, Fez swallowed, licked his lips, and let out a soft, "Mmm." He looked down at his hooves and waited for them to change—but nothing happened. "Why isn't it working?" he asked.

"Give it time," said Lou. "Even with pure garlic, it takes quite a bit for a transformation to wear off, so it will probably take a couple of hours with diluted garlic."

"Oh, okay," said Fez before letting out a small cough.

Ellie sprang to her feet and fanned Fez's garlic breath as she backed away. The white dressing bottle she held fell to the floor with a hollow plop.

Tink picked up the bottle and examined the label. "Fez, I thought you submitted your dad's entry to the contest?" He held up the bottle for everyone to see: "Fitzgerald's Garlic Dressing – Entry #21."

"I did, I mean…" Fez scrunched his face like he was trying to solve a very difficult math problem.

"If the entry bottle is here, what did you give to the judges?" Jessica asked. "The extra snack bottle?"

Ellie reached into her pocket and felt the sunglasses. She looked back at the dressing bottle, and then gasped. "Fez! I remember now! I left my sunglasses on your kitchen counter next to my sunscreen. You submitted my sunscreen to the contest!"

Fez's blue eyes began to bulge. "Oh no, the judges are going to eat your sunscreen!" He looked at the watch on his pink furry wrist. "And in only thirty minutes!"

Chapter Eleven
The Garlic Festival

The four friends ran as fast as their feet and hooves would carry them to the festival two blocks down. Since it was an outdoor event, Ellie needed something stronger than Tink's sunscreen, so she graciously accepted

when Lou offered her a bottle of the stinky formula. She smelled like a fresh fart mixed with flowers, but maybe the awful smell would mask the horrible scent of the Garlic Festival.

They waited in line to get into the gated park that was now fitted with large striped tents. Country music blared from the back speakers, and strings of colorful flags hung from all the large oak trees. Ellie turned to Fez, who was drooling over the poster for the garlic rib-eating contest. "How could you confuse my sunscreen for dressing?" She crossed her arms over her chest.

Fez turned toward her and timidly shrugged. "It was an accident. I'm so sorry. Both bottles were on the kitchen counter, so I thought my dad made an extra bottle. I guess I got distracted by the pie they were making on the Cooking Channel… I should have been paying more attention."

Ellie sighed. "It's okay. The bottles *do* look really similar." The group went silent until they reached the front of the line. Security checked their bags and then moved their attention toward Fez the Piglet. In the rush of the situation, they had completely forgotten that it wasn't normal to walk around as a pig.

They all stood perfectly still and held their breaths as the man looked over Fez. "Turn please," requested the security guard on the left. Fez spun in a circle, which showed off the curly little tail that had sprung from the back of his pants. To their relief, both guards broke out in a smile. "That's an amazing costume!"

said the guard. He waved the group in, and everyone let out a sigh of relief.

"Well, that could have gone horribly," said Tink.

"No kidding," Jessica agreed. "I kept thinking we were about to be arrested for having a pig as a friend." Everyone but Jessica laughed. "What, Fez turned into a pig today. Anything is possible!" she argued.

The park was packed with people of all ages, many younger kids toting around balloons with pictures of garlic on them. Fez pointed over the crowd to an area near the back of the festival, where there was a large wooden stage with purple satin curtains. "That's where the competition is," he explained. "Let's go!" They all followed Fez through the thick crowd of people. Between Fez's pig features and Ellie's horrible stench, they got more than enough weird looks. Ellie nervously chewed the inside of her cheek. What if people started calling her Smelly Ellie? That would be so much worse than Scaredy Bat. Her palms began to sweat.

They hit another security checkpoint, but unfortunately this time it didn't go as well. "Excuse me," said the guard, "this is a costume-only zone." He tapped the sign that said the same thing.

"We just need to reach the food competition and we'll be out in a flash," said Ellie.

"Nope, sorry." The guard pointed to Fez. "He can come in, but you guys can't."

Jessica looked at Fez. "Go in and save the sunscreen! We'll wait here." With a quick nod, Fez agreed and ran in. The trio silently waited on a bench nearby, and Ellie nervously chewed on her fingernails. What if she couldn't go on the trip and she missed meeting Hailey Haddie? Or even worse, what if Jessica took Ava as her partner and they became best friends? A loud cheering rose from the back of the festival.

"Hey, Ellie! I thought most vampires stayed away from here. What are you guys doing at the Garlic Festival?"

Ellie looked up to a familiar, soft voice and shrieked. *Poof!*

A clown stood in front of her with messy

blue hair, a soft pink face, and overly large red lips. It turned out clowns were even creepier when they knew your name.

"Oh no. Sorry. It's just me!" The clown took off her wig to reveal her long black hair and gave her best smile. Ellie hung from a tree upside down and fluttered right side up to get a better look. Her heartbeat slowed as she recognized Ava. *Poof!*

"You almost gave me a heart attack!" Ellie exclaimed.

"Sorry…" Ava said sheepishly. "I just wanted to say hi."

"I guess this explains the creepy clown stuff in your backpack," Jessica said.

"Yeah, I decided to volunteer to get to know the town a bit better."

Honk! Honk!

The sounds of a horn blasted through the air, and Ava threw her wig back on. "That's my cue!" she explained. "See you guys later."

No sooner had Ava gone than Fez emerged from the back area with something in his hand, and Ellie's heart felt like it was thumping a million beats per minute. He ran to the group and bent over to try to catch his breath.

"Did you get it?" Tink asked.

"Where is it?" Jessica inquired.

Ellie reached down at what Fez was holding and excitedly pulled it up to get a clear view. It was… a trophy? "This isn't my sunscreen!" Ellie cried.

Chapter Twelve
We Need a Plan

Fez took a deep breath. "No, we have a problem. They are doing a blind taste test, so all the labels were peeled off the bottles, and they all look similar. There are over a hundred of them! I need help to find the sunscreen bottle."

"That still doesn't explain the trophy," said Jessica.

Fez blushed. "I may have accidentally won the best costume competition. I was the crowd favorite!"

"We need a plan," said Tink. "Well, actually we need costumes." Just then, multiple clowns emerged from a nearby tent, and a lump caught in the back of Ellie's throat. She didn't understand why clowns were a thing.

They weren't funny, just scary.

"I have an idea!" exclaimed Jessica. "Let's go." Jessica led the gang into the clown tent, which Ellie agreed to enter only after finding out it was empty. The floor was littered with clown clothes and accessories. Everything from your classic rubber chickens to rainbow-colored wigs to miles of scarves. Jessica began pulling on a costume, and Tink followed her lead. Zipping up the front of a polka-dot jumpsuit over her dress, Jessica urged Ellie to join. "Come on, you need a costume to get in."

Ellie backed as far away from the clown accessories as she could, nearly ripping the soft fabric of the tent's back wall. "There's no way I am getting near clowns or their things. You'll have to do it without me."

Jessica threw a wig on her head, her red curls still spilling out from underneath. "We can't get through that many bottles without you, Ellie. And you're most likely to recognize the sunscreen. We need you." Both Fez and Tink agreed. Jessica walked over to Ellie and put on a red nose. "See, I'm a clown now, and it's still just me. Are you really scared of your best friend?"

Ellie took a moment before answering. "I guess it's just a costume…"

"Think of Hailey Haddie," Fez added.

Ellie reluctantly agreed and pulled on a clown costume. She supposed it was just like any other Halloween costume.

"Hey, does your necklace usually glow?" Tink asked, looking over at Ellie's dragon pendant.

"Not now, Tink," said Jessica. "We have sunscreen to save!"

The three clowns and the piglet frantically ran toward the testing table, only to discover it was too late—all the bottles were empty. With the threat of heavy rain in the forecast, the festival had moved the competition up an hour.

Fez gave a sad little oink. "I thought the

competition wasn't until later," he said. "I thought we still had time...."

"Well, that's that, I guess," Ellie said with a heavy sigh. No field trip, no Hailey Haddie, no fun. This school year was turning out to be the worst.

Chapter Thirteen
Lollipop Surprise

Ellie slumped down the gym wall as she watched the rest of her classmates excitedly chat about tomorrow's field trip to Jellyfish Lake—a trip that she would not be going on. She supposed being a shut-in until her new sunscreen arrived next month wasn't the worst thing in the world, though. It was far better than being called "Smelly Ellie," or whatever other nicknames her classmates would come up with. She would take Scaredy Bat over those any day.

"Ellie! Ellie!" came a small voice from the gym door. Tink, Fez, and Jessica were racing toward her.

"Oh. Hi guys," said Ellie as she tried to muster up a meek smile.

"We got you something," said Fez.

Jessica held out a purple gift bag with silver polka dots and a big pink bow.

"We think you'll like it," added Tink.

Ellie's small smile turned into a large grin as she took the bag from Jessica. She reached in and pulled out some sparkly tissue paper before finding a white-and-blue bottle. She squealed with joy. "How did you get this!? I can't believe…" Ellie trailed off as she read the label. "Fitzgerald's Garlic Dressing. Low in fat, big on taste."

"Isn't that cool!" said Fez. "My dad won the competition, all thanks to your sunscreen, and now his recipe is going to be in stores all over the country."

Ellie kept her eyes glued to the bottle, re-reading the label over and over. "That's great, Fez," she said in a monotone, almost robotic voice.

Jessica giggled. "Okay, guys, stop teasing her and give her the real gift."

Ellie looked up from the bottle for the first time. "Real gift?"

Tink unzipped his backpack and pulled out a few books, an old map, three packs of gum, and some wire. "Hold on, I know it's in here somewhere."

"Is there anything you don't have in there?" Jessica asked, placing her hands on her hips.

Ignoring the question, Tink kept digging. "Aha!" He proudly held up a simple white bottle. "*This* is your gift."

Ellie hesitantly took the bottle, her face scrunching up in confusion as she took in its plainness. Unlike the garlic dressing, this bottle didn't even have a label.

"It's Stinky Lou's sunscreen!" Fez exclaimed.

"But it doesn't smell bad anymore," added Jessica.

Ellie popped open the cap and was pleasantly surprised to be greeted with the sweet smell of lilacs. "Oh my gosh, this smells amazing! And it works?" she asked in disbelief.

"Yup!" Tink confirmed proudly. "Lou and I have been working really hard on it, and we finally figured it out. Plus, this won't just work for you; it's formulated to work for all vampires!"

Ellie's heart quickened with excitement. "Thank you so much!" She lunged toward Tink and wrapped her arms around him.

"I-I can't breathe," Tink gasped.

"Then you aren't going to like this!" Jessica jumped in to join the hug.

"Don't forget me!" said Fez, diving in too.

"Aw, look at the cute wittle group hug," taunted nearby Jack in a mocking baby voice.

They all looked around and glared at their new foe. "Jack, mind your own business," demanded Jessica.

Jack's eyes narrowed. "Make me!"

"Woah! Guys, we can all be friends." Tink reached into his backpack and started to unwrap a lollipop. Everyone looked at Tink, confused. "We can call a truce. Want to be our friend, Jack?" Jack looked down at the unwrapped blue lollipop, and the slight confusion on his face disappeared. He snatched the candy from Tink's hand and popped it in his mouth.

"Ha! Nope! I do want your candy, though. Thanks, dweeb!" And with that, Jack took off to the other side of the gym.

"Oh, I'm going to get him!" Jessica lurched forward, but Tink held her back.

"No, it's okay."

"You can't just let him steal your stuff like that, Tink!" Ellie exclaimed.

"Oh, I don't think he will be stealing anything for a while."

A loud scream sounded from the other side of the gym, and Jack emerged from a crowd of students... completely blue. Even his black curly hair was now the color of a Smurf. The

entire gym burst into laughter as Jack ran for the door.

"Oh my gosh, you turned him blue!?" Jessica exclaimed.

Tink gave a small smirk. "I told him I would when he took Fez's dressing."

As the four friends shared a laugh, Ellie couldn't believe her luck. Not only did she get to see Jack turn blue and could go on the field trip tomorrow, but she also had the best friends imaginable. Whatever mystery was in store for them next, she knew that if they worked together, nothing was unsolvable... Well, except maybe the mystery of why people liked garlic. That was something a Scaredy Bat like her would never understand.

Are You Afraid of Clowns?

Coulrophobia [kool-ruh-foh-bee-uh] is the extreme or irrational fear of clowns. It comes from the Greek word "kolon," meaning limb or stilts, which many clowns use in circus acts, and "phobos," the Greek word for fear.

Fear Rating: Coulrophobia is one of the less common phobias in the world. People with this phobia can get panic attacks, nausea, sweat excessively, cry, or scream at the sight of clowns.

Origin: Fear of clowns likely comes from their distorted features and not knowing their true emotion or identity. Popular media has also contributed to the fear.

Fear Facts:
- The word clown comes from "klunni," the Icelandic word for clumsy person.
- Clowning is a form of entertainment in virtually every culture.
- An early form of clown was the 'fool,' which traces back to ancient Egypt.
- Fools and jesters were often the only people in court who had free speech.
- International Clown Week is celebrated each year from August 1st - 7th.
- Trained clowns must follow 8 "Clown Commandments."

Jokes: What did the egg say to the clown? You crack me up!

Fear No More! Clowns are meant to be a source of entertainment, not fear. But if you believe you suffer from coulrophobia and want help, talk to your parents or doctor about treatment options. For more fear facts, visit: scaredybat.com/bundle1.

Suspect List

Fill in the suspects as you read, and don't worry if they're different from Ellie's suspects. When you think you've solved the mystery, fill out the "who did it" section on the next page!

Name: Write the name of your suspect
Motive: Write the reason why your suspect might have committed the crime
Access: Write the time and place you think it could have happened
How: Write the way they could have done it
Clues: Write any observations that may support the motive, access, or how

Suspect 1

Draw below

Name:
Motive:
Access:
How:
Clues:

Suspect 2

Draw below

Name:
Motive:
Access:
How:
Clues:

Suspect 3

Draw below

Name:
Motive:
Access:
How:
Clues:

Suspect 4

Draw below

Name:
Motive:
Access:
How:
Clues:

Who Did It?

Now that you've identified all of your suspects, it's time to use deductive reasoning to figure out who actually committed the crime! Remember, the suspect must have a strong desire to commit the crime (or cause the accident) and the ability to do so.

For more detective fun, visit:
scaredybat.com/bundle1

Name:
Motive:
Access:
How:
Clues:

Hidden Details
Observation Sheet
-- Level One --

1. What event is advertised in the flyer that Fez was holding?
2. What unfamiliar object did Ellie find in the backpack?
3. Who did Ellie accidentally swap backpacks with?
4. What happens when vampires go out in the sun without their special sunscreen?
5. Who did Ellie see digging in the trash at her school?
6. What did Ellie find in her sister Penny's room that looked like her sunscreen?
7. What did Jack take from Fez that Ellie confused for her sunscreen?
8. What animal did Fez turn into?
9. What's the problem with Lou's sunscreen formula?
10. What did Fez submit to the Garlic Festival for the tasting competition?

Hidden Details
Observation Sheet
-- Level Two --

1. What classroom number is Ellie's homeroom?
2. What is the name of Ellie's homeroom teacher?
3. What image is on Ellie's sunscreen bottle?
4. What did Tink give Ellie to protect her from the sun to get home?
5. What did Ellie use to cover her green splotches during dinner?
6. What image was on Fez's bottle of dressing?
7. What kind of animal is featured in the paintings at Lou's house?
8. What food can help Fez turn back into a human?
9. What does Fez win a trophy for?
10. What do the kids have to dress up as to get past the second guard at the festival?

Hidden Details
Observation Sheet
-- Level Three --

1. What kind of animal is stitched onto Ava's backpack?
2. Where is the class going for their upcoming field trip?
3. How often does Ellie get a new bottle of sunscreen?
4. What image is on the purple notepad Ellie uses to take notes about suspects?
5. What is the name of the movie that Jessica's mom is acting in?
6. What is Hailey Haddie doing in the photo in Ellie's room?
7. What does Tink's homemade temporary sunscreen smell like?
8. What was Lou trying to cure with his helmet?
9. Which vampire skin type does Ellie have?
10. What does Lou's new sunscreen smell like?

For more detective fun, visit:
scaredybat.com/bundle1

Level One Answers

1. The Garlic Festival
2. A clown mask
3. Ava
4. Blue spots; can drain transformation powers
5. Stinky Lou
6. Penny's sunscreen
7. Fitzgerald Garlic Dressing
8. A pig
9. It stinks
10. Ellie's sunscreen

Level Two Answers

1. 302
2. Mr Bramble
3. Sun with a straw hat and red sunglasses
4. Tinfoil
5. A purple scarf
6. A yellow garlic head wearing red sunglasses
7. A cat
8. Garlic
9. Costume contest
10. Clowns

Level Three Answers

1. Lion
2. Jellyfish Lake
3. Once a month
4. Silver skeleton key
5. Vampires in Paradise
6. Chewing a pen cap as she made a list of suspects
7. Black licorice
8. Hiccups
9. Skin type 4B
10. Lilacs

Answer Key

Questions for Discussion

1. What did you enjoy about this book?
2. What are some of the major themes of this story?
3. Who was your favorite character? What did you like about him/her?
4. How did the characters use their strengths to solve the mystery together?
5. Have you ever experienced bullying? What happened?
6. What fears did the characters express in the book? When have you been afraid? How have you dealt with your fears?
7. What is your favorite red colored food?
8. What other books, shows, or movies does this story remind you of?
9. What do you think will happen in the next book in the series?
10. If you could talk to the author, what is one question you would ask her?

For more discussion questions, visit:
scaredybat.com/bundle1

ScaredyBat
and the Missing Jellyfish

By Marina J. Bowman

Illustrated by Yevheniia Lisovaya

Scaredy Bat
AND THE MISSING JELLYFISH

1. A Jerky Bus Ride 221
2. The Wonders of Jellyfish Lake.........229
3. I Spy With My Little Eye.................237
4. Jinx! 243
5. RIP Mr. Frog 250
6. Tale of the Hairy Toe........................258
7. Sloosh! Gurgle! Glug! 267
8. Footprints In The Sand 273
9. Cabin in the Woods...........................280
10. Rat, Bat, Cat, or Worm....................287
11. Jelly Belly 295
12. Ready Yeti 304
13. Little Ballerinas..................................309
14. Wishes And Dreams 315
15. An Invitation 324

Batty Bonuses

Are You Afraid of Deep Waters? 334
Suspect List 336
Who Did It? 341
Hidden Observation Details Sheet 342
Discussion Questions 347

Can you solve the mystery?

All you need is an eye for detail, a sharp memory, and good logical skills. Join Ellie on her mystery-solving adventure by making a suspect list and figuring out who committed the crime! To help with your sleuthing, you'll find a suspect list template and hidden details observation sheets at the back of the book.

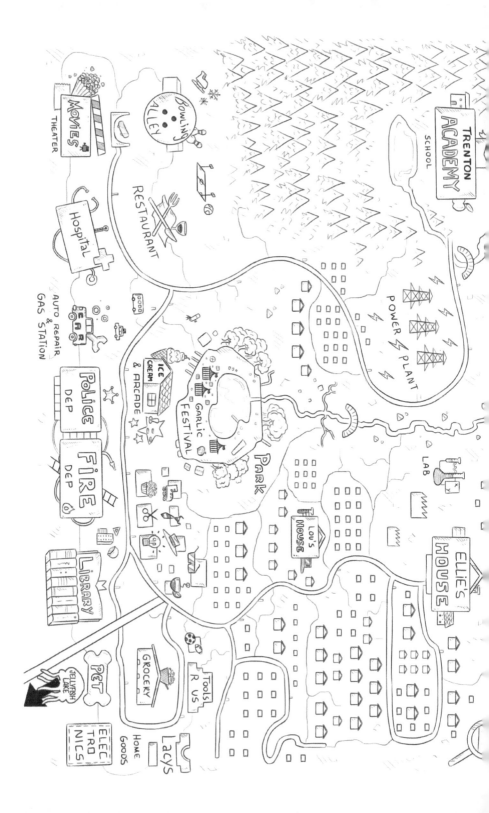

*There's a place not far from here
With strange things 'round each corner
It's a town where vampires walk the streets
And unlikely friendships bloom*

*When there's a mystery to solve
Ellie Spark is the vampire to call
Unless she's scared away like a cat
Poof! There goes that Scaredy Bat*

*Villains and pesky sisters beware
No spider, clown, or loud noise
Will stop Ellie and her team
From solving crime, one fear at a time*

Chapter One
A Jerky Bus Ride

TUNK!
The school bus hit a large bump, spilling the contents of Ellie's pink backpack across the aisle. With a groan, Ellie scooped up her pajamas, bathing suit, detective notepad, and some snacks—everything she needed for the overnight class trip to Jellyfish Lake. She stuffed it all back into her bag, but something very important was missing.

"My sunscreen!" Ellie said with a gasp. "No, no, no. This can't be happening again." She leaned down to look under the seat, but all she found was a dust bunny and wads of chewed bubble gum.

"Found it!" came a cheerful voice. Ellie

flipped back up to face the round, smiling face of one of her best friends, Fez. He extended the sunscreen toward Ellie across the aisle.

With a sigh of relief, she grabbed it and gently placed it into her backpack. "Thank you!" Ellie said, but Fez's attention was now somewhere else. In his other hand, he held a stick of wrinkled meat sheathed in plastic.

"Jelly Belly Liver Jam Jerky," he read off the label. "If it doesn't make you feel perky, it isn't Jelly Belly Jerky." Fez's eyes grew wide with excitement. "Well, that's one delicious tongue twister," he exclaimed, licking his lips.

"Go ahead," said Ellie, stifling a small giggle. She'd never expected someone to look so jazzed about jam jerky. But she supposed if anyone were going to be excited about jelly-filled meat, it would be Fez. He eagerly tore into the package and took a big bite out of the meat stick. A stream of green jelly promptly squirted out, giving the bat design on his t-shirt a goopy beard. But Fez didn't seem to notice.

"This is soooo good," he exclaimed. "It's salty, tangy, and…" He licked his lips. "Just a little bit sweet. How have I never had this before!?"

"I think only the vampire grocery stores have it," explained Ellie. "And it's pretty new. I haven't even tried it yet."

Fez popped the last piece of gooey meat into his mouth just as she spoke.

"Oops." He held up the empty wrapper and gave a big swallow. "Sorry."

Ellie laughed. "That's okay. I have more! They're also coming out with a glowing jelly next month! I can't wait to make a glowing bone marrow butter and jelly sandwich." Ellie's mouth watered at the thought. She dug in her backpack for another meat stick just as Jessica walked to the back of the bus.

Jessica's red curls bounced as she plopped down beside Ellie and exhaled dramatically. "Please tell me you haven't lost your sunscreen again," Jessica said with an eye roll as she watched Ellie shuffle around the contents of her backpack. "I do not want to waste our field trip to Jellyfish Lake looking for sunscreen. Or hearing you complain about turning blue from the sun."

Before Ellie could even respond to her oldest friend's curiously catty comment, Fez chimed in from across the aisle. "I still think it's so odd that you vampires can permanently turn blue from too much sun, or even lose your transformational powers. Crazy."

"No, what's really crazy is how long this drive is taking," Jessica complained. "We've been on this bus forever."

"Why are you so crabby?" Ellie asked.

Jessica wrinkled her nose. "Gah. I'm not. This is just the longest bus ride ever. I want to get off of this hot sticky bus and swim."

"Me, too!" agreed Fez. "I think I want to write my report about swimming with jellyfish. It was one of the ideas on the handout."

Fez smoothed out a crumpled sheet he pulled from his pocket.

Grade 7 – Jellyfish Lake Report

Ideas to get you started:

1. *Your personal experience swimming in Jellyfish Lake. It should be unique, since this is one of the only lakes in the world where you can swim with jellyfish.*
2. *Tourism and how it supports the Jellyfish Lake Science Camp and preservation of the lake.*
3. *The lake's history. These beaches are where the Fang and Flesh Treaty was first signed. Vampires and humans lived in harmony here long before it became more widespread.*
4. *The ecosystem and animals surrounding the lake.*
5. *Of course, you are welcome to use your own ideas, but these should get those brain juices flowing.*

Happy swimming!

Ellie got to the last line, and her breath caught in her throat.

"I am *not* going swimming," she declared.

"Why not!?" asked Fez. "The best part about Jellyfish Lake is you can swim with the jellyfish."

Ellie looked around the bus at all the other kids, who were enthusiastically chatting away. She leaned over Jessica toward Fez and lowered her voice to a whisper.

"I'm scared of swimming in lakes."

"What?" Fez asked.

Ellie cleared her throat and said it slightly louder, her cheeks getting warm. "I'm scared of swimming in lakes."

"What? I can't hear you," said Fez.

"Oh, for the love of pudding!" erupted Jessica. "She said she is scared of swimming in lakes!" She lowered her voice to a mutter. "She's called Scaredy Bat for a reason."

The kids in neighboring seats turned to look at the commotion. Ellie's face burned hot, and she sank down in the seat to avoid their gazes. The back of the blue bus seat may have been able to shield her from their judging looks, but it couldn't protect her from their giggles and whispers. Ellie clapped her hands over her ears.

SCREEEECH! Ellie jerked forward as the bus came to a hard stop. The squeal of the bus's brakes pierced through her makeshift hand earmuffs.

"Did you see that!?" bellowed the bus driver. "There was a monster! A big brown furry one, right in the middle of the road."

Chapter Two
The Wonders of Jellyfish Lake

Everyone stood to try to catch a glimpse of the monster. Out of the corner of her eye, Ellie spotted a large, rustling bush through the smudged bus window. But when she turned for a better look, the bush was still. *Could there really be a monster?* she wondered.

As if reading Ellie's thoughts, Mr. Bramble's deep voice boomed over the commotion. "Sit down, everyone. Sit down," he urged in the same loud voice he used when teaching. "There is nothing to see. It was probably just a bear—certainly not a monster." Mr. Bramble turned toward the bus driver and gave a deep sigh, clearly unimpressed that he had caused such a fright.

The bus driver, who had big round glasses that made his eyes look like an owl's, only gave a slight shrug. "But I could have sworn I saw—"

"Please return to your seats so we can get on our way," Mr. Bramble interrupted. "We should only be about ten minutes out from the camp now."

Ellie's heart thumped hard against the wall of her chest as she slid back down in her seat and propped her knees up. Her embarrassment was quickly overtaken by thoughts of what the bus driver saw. What if there really was a monster? Or was Mr. Bramble right, and it was just a bear? Ellie knew exactly who to ask. She scooted past Jessica and walked to the front of the bus. Right in the front seat was a boy with curly brown hair and glasses. He had his face buried in a large book.

"Hey, Tink," Ellie said, sitting in the seat behind him. "Why are you all the way up here?"

Tink lifted his face out of the book and smiled.

"Oh, hey, Ellie. I just wanted some quiet to read." He turned his book cover toward her and pointed to the title: *The Wonders of Jellyfish Lake*. "Have you read this?" he asked. "It's absolutely fascinating." Before Ellie could answer, Tink continued, "For example, did you know that jellyfish have no eyes, bones, brains, or hearts? They are made mostly of water. And the type of jellyfish found in Jellyfish Lake don't sting, which is why it's such a popular tourist attraction. And freshwater jellyfish are in danger due to pollution. And jellyfish have—"

Ellie interrupted, knowing that Tink could go on all day about the facts he'd learned. "Does that book say anything about"—Ellie lowered her voice to a whisper—"any brown and furry monsters?"

Tink adjusted his glasses on his nose and thumbed through a few pages.

"Hmm, so far it hasn't, but I'm only about halfway through."

Ellie nibbled on her nails. Tink offered her a smile and lowered his voice. "You know, what the bus driver saw was probably just a bear, or even a moose. And have you seen the size of his glasses? I don't know how he drives, let alone identifies a monster."

Ellie looked up at the bus driver, who had earphones stuffed in his ears. His glasses really were thick. She watched as a fly landed on his nose, and he smacked himself in the face. The fly buzzed away and landed on Ellie's turquoise trench coat. Ellie and Tink both snickered.

"Thanks, Tink," Ellie said, sighing with relief.

Mr. Bramble got to his feet a few seats away and hushed the class.

"If I can have everyone's attention, I have a little surprise. By now, you all know about the presentation and report you have to do on Jellyfish Lake. The fact that it's worth thirty percent of your grade should be enough incentive to do your best work. But as a bonus, there will be a prize for the top three projects."

Everyone on the bus started whispering about what it could be. Ellie's classmates guessed everything from a new bike to a pass for the new amusement park.

Mr. Bramble hushed the class once again. "The three best projects will get to go to Jellyfish Lake!" The class became silent.

"Isn't that where we're going?" asked a girl with two green braids.

"Right you are," said Mr. Bramble. "But the winners will get a spot at Jellyfish Lake's Science Camp this year, with special guest counselor Bonnie Samson." The class remained silent, but Mr. Bramble didn't seem to notice

the lack of enthusiasm. "So you better start thinking about those projects!"

Ellie groaned. "I should have known any surprise by Mr. Bramble would be lame," she whispered to Tink.

"Lame!?" Tink said in genuine shock. "Bonnie Samson is anything but lame. She is absolutely amazing."

"Who is that?" Ellie asked.

"You don't know who Bonnie Samson is!?" Ellie shrugged.

"She is an amazing scientist. She figured out how to isolate the invisibility gene in ghosts and is running tests on how to apply it to different species."

"That's pretty neat," Ellie said genuinely, but apparently not with enough excitement to satisfy Tink.

"Pretty neat? Let me put it this way," Tink tried again. "I feel about Bonnie Samson how you feel about Hailey Haddie." Now *that* Ellie fully understood. She didn't know what she would do if she ever got to meet her hero, actress Hailey Haddie. AKA the best vampire detective ever.

"Wow, you must really like her!" Ellie concluded. "I wish there was a way I could meet Hailey Haddie."

Tink nodded enthusiastically. "Like I said, AMAZING. Now, I really have to finish this book."

"Okay. Well, come sit with us if you get sick of reading."

Tink laughed. "I don't think I could ever get sick of reading!" Tink lifted his book back up to his face. "Especially not this chapter; it talks about how there are half a million jellyfish in Jellyfish Lake."

"That's a lot! Are there really that many?" Ellie asked.

Tink was now fully immersed in his book and didn't hear Ellie.

Mr. Bramble cleared his throat as Ellie stood. "Actually, there aren't quite that many jellyfish anymore," he explained. "In fact, I got an email this morning saying that many seem to be going missing lately."

"Oh, where do you think they're going?" Ellie asked.

Mr. Bramble furrowed his brow. "Not sure. It's a real mystery."

Ellie let out a large gasp, and her eyes widened. If this was a mystery, then she was on the case!

Chapter Three
I Spy With My Little Eye

Ellie pranced back to her seat as Jessica scooted to the spot closest to the window. Ellie would tell her friends about the case later, but first, she wanted to find a lead.

"Ooo! Wanna play I Spy?" asked Fez as soon as he spotted Ellie. "I'm great at this game." Without waiting for Ellie to sit, or even agree, Fez began. "I spy with my little eye something that is brown."

Jessica sat in silence as Ellie played along while she dug for her notebook. She guessed everything from Jessica's sweater to the gunk stuck on the bus's windowsill. But after several minutes, she still couldn't figure it out.

"I give up," Ellie said eventually as her

stomach gave a monstrous growl. "I'm too hungry and distracted. What is it?" She reached in her backpack and searched for a stick of jerky.

"It's the mark on Jessica's arm! It kind of looks like a mouse," said Fez with a big grin.

But when Ellie turned to see what he was talking about, Jessica had already tugged the

leopard-print sleeve down to hide the brown spot. She sprang to her feet and looked at Ellie, who had finally found the Jelly Belly Liver Jam Jerky.

"If you're going to eat that disgusting thing, I'm going to sit somewhere else," Jessica scoffed. She paused for a second to stifle a sneeze before climbing over Ellie and making her way to an empty seat a few rows back. Ellie and Fez shared a confused glance. Jessica was never afraid to speak her mind, but she wasn't normally mean about it—especially not to her best friend, Ellie.

"It definitely seems like something is bugging Jessica," said Fez as Ellie turned to look at Jessica, who was staring out the window in her new seat.

"Definitely," Ellie agreed. It was odd that she was so crabby. And why would she be wearing a sweater on the bus when she said she was hot earlier? Ellie's stomach growled once again, interrupting her thoughts. Ellie gave her mopey-looking friend one last glance before turning her attention to her notebook.

After a few minutes of scribbling, though, she hadn't gotten very far—she'd only managed to doodle a jellyfish and a blank numbered list of clues and suspects.

Ellie's stomach grumbled once more. *Maybe I just need some food*, she thought. She finally peeled open the stick of jerky, but before she could take a bite, it was gone.

SCREEEECH! The jerky flew out of her hand as the bus once again came to a sudden stop.

Not another monster, Ellie thought.

"Oops," said the bus driver. "Hit the brakes a bit too hard that time. Sorry! But we're here."

Fez pointed to the Jam Jerky on the ground. "Are you going to eat that?"

Ellie looked at a dust bunny near her snack and slumped her shoulders.

"No. Go ahead."

Fez scooped it off the ground and gave it a good blow before chomping down.

Everyone slowly poured out of the bus onto the pink-and-white gravel pathway that forked off to the cabins, beach, and trails. Ellie fanned

her face as the hot sun beat down. She grabbed her sunscreen and slathered it on, but soon her hands became too slippery. The bottle popped right out of her grip and rolled under the bus to the other side. Ellie walked around the bus but paused to watch a stout man and a woman in deep conversation. They both wore beige and green park ranger outfits.

"The jellyfish are just vanishing," said the plump park ranger. "If this continues, we're going to have to close the park—possibly for good."

"That's terrible," said the slender woman. "Why would we have to close the park?"

"We need to preserve the jellyfish that are left," the plump ranger explained. "With them disappearing, the whole lake's ecosystem is in danger."

"Where do you think all the jellyfish are going?"

"No idea. But between the disappearing jellyfish and those strange footprints on the beach last week, this place sure is weird lately."

"Yes!" Ellie cheered, far louder than intended. This was the lead she needed.

The two park rangers turned toward her.

"Oh, um. I…" Ellie spotted her sunscreen on the gravel near her feet. "My sunscreen!" she pointed at it. "I wasn't sure where it went, but I found it. Yippee." Ellie quickly scooped up her sunscreen and raced to tell her friends about their new case.

Chapter Four
Jinx!

When Ellie got to the other side of the bus, the class was already walking to the cabins. She ran up the line and soon found Fez and Tink. "Psst. Guys, you will never guess what." Ellie explained to them what she had just heard and how they had a mystery on their hands.

A loud snort sounded behind her just as she finished her explanation. Ellie turned around to face her least favorite person ever, Jack Grinko. A new kid this year who seemed to love making people miserable, especially Ellie and her friends.

"Look at the little Scaredy Bat making up stories. It's cute that you and your wittle friends

still play make-belief." Jack laughed.

Ellie put her hands on her hips. "I am not making this up. And I wasn't even talking to you."

Mr. Bramble clapped his hands from the front of the line, which had now come to a stop. "Miss Spark!" he shouted. "If you were listening at all, which clearly you were not, you would know that this is the line for the boy's cabin. Are you a boy?" Ellie took a good look at the line of boys. She shook her head. Mr. Bramble pointed to another line a few cabins

down. "Then that is where you need to be."

Ellie mumbled an apology before sprinting to her lineup. She looked up and down it for Jessica, but she was nowhere in sight.

Half an hour later, after unpacking and getting into her yellow-and-blue-striped swimsuit, Ellie found herself squidging the soft, warm sand between her toes. She took in the sight of the clear turquoise lake lined with trees and cabins. She got just close enough to the lake so that the gentle waves and cool water could lick her toes—but that was as far as she would

go. She took in a deep breath, and the earthy smell of pine tickled her nostrils.

"ACHOO!" Ellie let out a big sneeze, followed by another. "ACHOO!"

"Sanalamia!" said a cheerful voice from behind Ellie. Ellie turned toward her classmate, Ava Grinko, lying on a beach chair in her purple ruffled swimsuit and oversized sunglasses. Ellie looked down at her old swimsuit and felt frumpy in comparison.

"Thanks!" said Ellie.

"You're welcome. If you're going to go for a swim, I would be happy to watch your necklace so you don't lose it," Ava offered with a big, fangy smile.

"No thanks," Ellie replied as she thumbed the purple dragon necklace that hung around her neck. A soft, cool wave washed over her foot, and she backed away. "I don't really like swimming in lakes," she added.

"Ah, me neither. It always tangles my hair," Ava said as she twirled one of her shiny black ringlets. "Let me know if you change your mind!"

Ellie smiled and nodded. "I will. Thanks!"

Ellie watched Tink and Fez in the lake. They'd decided that the two boys should go see exactly how many jellyfish there were firsthand and look for any clues. However, right now, it sure seemed like they were playing more than anything. They splashed each other, and Ellie wished she could join them. She had so much fun playing with them in the pool during the summer, but pools were safe. She knew how deep the pool was and that no monsters were lurking in the depths. The lake, on the other hand… well, anything could be in there.

Turning her attention back to the mystery, Ellie scanned the beach for any hint of mysterious creatures. But all she found were some neat rocks, a broken sandcastle shovel, a few chip bags, and some plastic bottles.

Where could the jellyfish be going? she thought. Ellie remembered what the bus driver had seen and what the park rangers said. *What if there was a lake monster, and what if he was also able to walk on the land?* However, she hadn't found

any strange footprints herself, so who knew what the ranger had seen. She wandered further down the beach.

SPLAT!

Ellie's sandal was pulled down by an orange sticky mess beside a soda can.

"Ew!" Ellie cried.

Fez and Tink emerged from the lake just in time to watch Ellie try to free her sandal from the sticky spot.

Tink scrunched up his face. "What did you step in?"

Ellie tried to wipe the orange gunk off, but her sandal just picked up more sand. She pointed to the soda can.

"Orange soda that has been cooking in the hot sun," she said.

"Ewww," said Fez and Tink at the same time.

"Jinx!" exclaimed Fez. "You owe me a…" He looked at the sticky, gross mess on the ground. "Well, maybe not a soda."

"I can't stand people who litter," said Tink. "Don't they know it pollutes the lake?"

"That's it!" exclaimed Ellie. "Tink, you're a genius. I have a new lead for the case!"

"I am pretty smart, but what did I say?" asked Tink.

But Ellie was already rushing to the lake.

Chapter Five
RIP Mr. Frog

Tink and Fez followed Ellie to the lake.

"Look at all the garbage," Ellie said. She pointed at bottles and cans littering the beach, along with aluminum wrappers and plastic packaging. "Earlier, you told me that jellyfish are in danger due to pollution, so isn't it possible that there are fewer jellyfish because the lake is polluted?"

"Yes, that is possible," agreed Tink.

"Look!" Ellie pointed to a frog that was belly-up on the shore.

"I'm going to go get my water testing kit from my backpack," Tink said. "That should help us figure out if pollution is causing this."

Soon Tink rushed back with a plastic

briefcase. He popped open the latches and pulled out a thin, white strip of paper.

"What does that do?" Fez asked.

"It will tell us the pH of the water," Tink responded. Ellie and Fez gave him a blank look. "It will tell us if the lake is too acidic or not acidic enough. Both can hurt fish. I made these test strips out of red cabbage juice and coffee filters, so they aren't as accurate as real pH strips, but they should give us an idea." Tink dipped the test strip into the lake water, and it turned a medium green.

"What does that mean?" asked Fez.

Tink pulled out a chart with a color scale that ranged from red to purple. It was also numbered 1 to 14. He held the test strip up to match the color.

"Looks like a seven," said Ellie. "Is that okay?"

"That is perfect. It means the water is neutral. If it were pink-ish red, it would mean it was acidic like a lemon. If it had turned purple-ish, then it would have been non-acidic, also known as a base, like soapy water."

"That's really neat!" Ellie exclaimed. "So you can figure out if the lake is polluted just by testing the pH of the water?"

"Not quite," answered Tink. "I wish it was that simple. PH is only one part of lake health, but besides the litter, the lake looks healthy. I was actually reading in my book today that Jellyfish Lake has some of the cleanest water in this region."

Fez turned to the frog. "What do you think happened to this guy, then?"

Tink shrugged. "Could have been too hot for him, maybe he got wounded, or maybe it was just his time."

"Poor little guy," said Fez. Fez plucked a yellow flower from a grassy patch and laid it down on the frog. "Rest in peace, Mr. Frog."

RIBBIT! The frog rolled over onto his feet and hopped toward the tall grass.

"Or I guess he could just be sleeping," said Tink.

They all laughed.

"Well, it doesn't look like pollution is to blame," Ellie said. "Did you guys see anything weird while you were swimming?"

Tink scratched his chin. "Now that I think about it, I only saw jellyfish here and there. It wasn't full of jellyfish like my book shows. In fact, there wasn't a smack anywhere."

Fez's eyes lit up. "Woah, a snack? There was supposed to be a snack?"

Tink snickered. "No, Fez. A *smack*. It's what you call a group of jellyfish."

"They should make a jelly candy called a smack snack!" declared Fez. "I would totally eat it."

"Fez, what wouldn't you eat?" Tink asked.

"Jellyfish, or frogs, or green apples."

Ellie cleared her throat. "Back to the mystery. So, there are definitely fewer jellyfish."

"Yes," Tink confirmed.

"Hey, have you seen Jessica?" Fez asked Ellie as he glanced down the beach. "I haven't seen her since we got here."

Ellie shook her head. "She eventually showed up in the girls' cabin earlier, but she was ignoring me for the most part."

A piercing scream echoed over the lake. All three of the friends looked at each other.

"Jessica!?"

They turned around, expecting to see their friend. But it was Ava standing on her beach chair. They rushed over to see what the commotion was about.

"What's going on?" asked Mr. Bramble. "Are you okay?"

Ava let out a small whimper. "I am not okay!"

"Are you hurt?" asked Mr. Bramble.

"Worse," said Ava. "There's a rat! A big furry rat that just ran across the beach."

Ellie turned a ghostly white.

"That's all?" Mr. Bramble asked. "I thought it was--"

The brown rat scurried across Ellie's foot, and she shrieked. With a dash and a hop, she joined Ava on the chair.

Mr. Bramble ran his hand over his face. "Miss Grinko, I realize you are used to your cushy city life that is free of pests. But please, try to calm down. Screaming at the top of your lungs is uncalled for. And that also goes for you, Miss Spark," he added, looking at Ellie. "The campfire is in ten minutes, so go to your cabin and start getting ready." With an exasperated sigh, Mr. Bramble walked away, and many of the curious onlookers followed.

Ellie and Ava hopped off their chairs and looked around.

"Do you think it's gone?" Ava asked.

"Yeah, I saw it run up the hill toward the cabins," said Ellie.

"Looks like Scaredy Bat is starting to rub off on you," Jack called from across the beach.

"Jack!" Ava shrieked. "Don't you have anything better to do?"

Jack repeated what his sister had said in a mocking voice before taking off to his cabin.

Tink rolled his eyes. "I should turn him blue again." A week before Jack had snatched a lollipop from him that turned him blue.

Ava giggled. "This time, you should try purple! I think that would look great on him."

Tink looked at the ground and lowered his voice. "Oh, umm…" He used his foot to trace lines in the sand. "Yeah, that would look good on him."

Ellie looked at the sand and spotted a wrapper for Jelly Belly Liver Jam Jerky. Her stomach rumbled. She couldn't wait for campfire marshmallows. She picked up the wrapper and walked to the garbage can. Almost all of the trash in the can was Jelly Belly brand. Soda cans, chip bags, plastic bottles—they were all from Jelly Belly.

Chapter Six
Tale of the Hairy Toe

Ellie was delighted to find Jessica in bed back at the cabin. Ellie wanted to fill her in on the case of the missing jellyfish, including the newest discovery of how all the beach garbage was from the same food company. It could be a clue.

"Where have you been?" Ellie asked.

"Around," Jessica replied.

"Around where?"

"We are miles away from anywhere fun, so obviously around here," snapped Jessica.

"Jess, I know you've been excited for this trip. You even said on the bus you wanted to swim, but I didn't see you at the beach. Where

have you been? And why are you suddenly being so crabby?"

"I'm not being crabby!"

"Then you might want to know we have a new mystery," Ellie said. "And you missed looking for clues and testing the water for pollution."

"Not everything is about mysteries, Ellie."

Before Ellie could respond, the rest of the girls in her class came in to change for the campfire. Ellie pulled on her clothes, including her turquoise trench coat for extra warmth.

"Want to walk with me to the campfire?" Ellie asked Jessica.

"I don't feel well right now. I'll catch up later," Jessica answered.

"Is it your allergies? The pine smell makes me sneeze, too. Is there anything I can do?"

Jessica pulled the fleece blanket over her head. "Just leave me alone."

"Okay," said Ellie as she tried to fight back tears. "I hope you feel better soon... Love you lots." Ellie left the cabin with Ava in tow.

"You think she will be okay?" Ava asked.

"I hope so," said Ellie, wiping a tear off her cheek. "I've known her since I was four, and I've seen her sick in the past. But she was never mean about it." What could possibly be going on with Jessica? Would she ever have her best friend back?

The sweet smell of melted marshmallows filled the air around the campfire. The entire class sat on wooden benches by the fire while chatting and roasting hotdogs, veggie dogs, and marshmallows. Ellie was excited to finally get some food, since she had been hungry since the bus. She wiped a glob of ketchup off the end of her hotdog before digging in. Tink, however, was far more interested in the wonders of nature and hadn't even touched his veggie dog.

Tink pointed to the dark sky, blanketed in millions of glowing stars. "Look, there's the Big Dipper! And there's the Little Dipper," he said.

"Wow, this is way prettier than the stars at home," said Fez, putting another marshmallow on his stick.

"Much less light pollution," Tink explained.

Ellie shoved the last of her hotdog in her mouth as she flipped open her detective notepad. She scribbled a list by the warm glow of the fire.

Possible clues:
> 1. The monster or bear the bus driver saw - maybe bears eat jellyfish?

2. *The footprints the park ranger was talking about – didn't find any myself.*
   3. *Garbage by the lake - all Jelly Belly?*

Suspects:
   1. *Pollution – kills many animals, and there is garbage around the lake*
   2. *Jack – he's such a bully. Maybe he bullied the jellyfish away!*
   3. *Someone who needs the jellyfish for something... but who?*

She tapped her pencil on her notepad and rethought her suspect list.
   1. *~~Pollution~~ – (The water tested fine and the frog wasn't dead.)*
   2. *~~Jack~~ – (The jellyfish went missing before he arrived. But he's still a big bully!)*
   3. *Someone who needs the jellyfish for something... but who?*

Ellie nibbled on her lip while she pondered what possible connection this could all have to the disappearing jellyfish. Who would need jellyfish and why? Maybe an aquarium ran out? Or perhaps they were worth a lot of money?

Mr. Bramble soon interrupted her thoughts. "Attention, everyone. I just got some bad news that you all need to hear. Unfortunately, Jellyfish Lake will be closing after this weekend, so the Science Camp is no longer available as a prize. So sorry to let you down. The park has decided that with all the jellyfish disappearing, it is best to protect those that are left."

He paused to let the class react, but no one seemed to care much—no one but Tink. Tink's mouth hung open as he stared at the fire.

"However, I think it is only fair that there is still a prize," Mr. Bramble continued. "So, the winner will now be getting tickets to the opening of the new theme park, Mega Adventure Land."

Everyone in the class started chatting excitedly about the new theme park and how they really wanted the tickets.

"Are you okay?" Fez asked Tink.

After a few seconds, Tink finally answered. "That Science Camp was my dream. My foster mom Shayla tried to get me in last year, but they only offer spots sponsored by schools

or companies. Not just anyone can join." He hung his head in his hands.

"If we can find what's happening to the jellyfish before we leave tomorrow, maybe you can still go," Ellie whispered.

Tink whipped his head up. "Then we need to find those jellyfish."

ACHOO!

A sneeze came from the dark forest, and to Ellie's shock and delight, Jessica stepped out and sat by the fire. Even though she sat far away, Ellie was still happy Jessica seemed to be feeling better.

"I think it is time for a spooky story before bed," said Miss Millotto, a short woman with gray hair and a twinkle in her eye. "I have been chaperoning this trip for a couple decades now, so I know a thing or two. Are you ready?"

The fire dimmed eerily.

"Once there was an old woman collecting mushrooms and berries in the forest around Jellyfish Lake. After little luck on her hunt, she finally stumbled upon a huge, juicy mushroom and was delighted that she would have

something to put in her soup. Except once the woman picked up the mushroom, she realized it wasn't a mushroom at all—it was a big, fat, hairy toe the size of her fist. With her stomach rumbling from hunger, she decided it would have to do and took it back to her small cabin on the edge of Jellyfish Lake."

"That night, she made some soup with the giant toe and went to bed with a full stomach. But around midnight, the door to her cabin slowly opened. *CREAK*! And there stood a big hairy silhouette that was eight-feet-tall. The woman was never seen again, but there were footprints found in her cabin. Massive footprints with the left foot missing a big toe."

With a slightly shaky hand, Ellie reached into her backpack, pulled out a stick of Jelly Belly Liver Jam Jerky, and peeled back the wrapper. *It's just a story; it's not real. It's just a scary story*, she told herself.

Suddenly, the leaves on the round bush behind Ellie started to rustle.

Chapter Seven
Sloosh! Gurgle! Glug!

Ellie's heart pounded faster at the sound of the moving leaves. She tried to remind herself it was probably just a rabbit or a squirrel, but then something grabbed her ankle.

"EEK!" Ellie shrieked as she dropped her jerky.

POOF! She flew into a nearby tree.

Jack crawled out of the bush and laughed. "Such a Scaredy Bat!"

"What is wrong with you!?" shouted Jessica from the other side of the campfire.

"Yeah, don't you have anything better to do?" said Fez.

"Nothing is wrong with me. I'm hilarious. And the better question is, why can't you ever

get food in your mouth instead of on your shirt?" Jack pointed to the green stain left by the Liver Jam Jerky earlier.

Poof! Ellie transformed back into a vampire. "You're just a big bully!" she shouted.

"And you're just a wannabe vampire detective. You and your little friends will never solve

any real mysteries." Jack changed his voice as if he were talking to a baby. "Is little bitty Scaredy Bat scared again? Boohoo!"

Tink stood. "Hey, Grinko," he called in a voice that was a bit too quiet. When Jack couldn't hear over his maniacal laughter, Tink tried again in a louder voice. "Jack! Leave her alone. What did she ever do to you?"

Before Jack could answer, Mr. Bramble cut in. "Enough!" he yelled. "Why is it always this group that I have to deal with? Mr. Grinko—"

SLOOSH! GURGLE! GLUG! GLUG! A loud slurping sound echoed through the chilly night air.

Jack's face went pale. "Okay, that isn't me this time."

They looked down at the lake, which was now a large whirlpool with spinning water sloshing everywhere. Then, just as soon as the water vortex had started, it stopped, and the lake calmed into soft waves. The class broke out into a tidal wave of whispers and theories.

"Probably just an underwater spring or

something," assured Mr. Bramble. "Come along now; it's time for bed."

Jessica rushed to Ellie. "Does this have anything to do with the mystery you were telling me about?"

"Yes!" exclaimed Ellie. She explained about the jellyfish, what they had found so far, and how they needed to solve this so Tink could go to Science Camp. "We need to get down there and look for clues," Ellie finished.

Tink and Fez both agreed, but Jessica remained silent.

"Do you think you're feeling well enough to join?" asked Ellie hopefully.

"Umm," said Jessica.

Fez picked up the Jelly Belly Liver Jam Jerky that Ellie had dropped when she turned into a bat. He looked at her with puppy dog eyes.

"Well, I'm not eating it," Ellie said, looking at the layer of dirt on it before turning her attention back to Jessica.

Fez blew it off, possibly releasing more spit than air.

Jessica stifled a sneeze. "No, I'll sit this one out," she finally answered.

Ellie's shoulders slumped as she watched Jessica take off down the hill. She'd thought for sure she was going to say yes. Fez shoved the rest of the jerky in his mouth and put a hand on Ellie's back.

"It's okay," he said. "Maybe she'll join us next time."

Ellie hoped he was right.

After the final headcount of the day, the three friends snuck down to the beach to search for more clues. They walked along the calm water's edge looking for anything out of the ordinary, but even with their flashlights and the light of the moon, it was hard to see.

"Ow," said Ellie as her foot hit something. A big long tooth was lying in the sand.

Chapter Eight
Footprints In The Sand

"Charybdis!" said Ellie. "I bet you she is behind this." Ellie stood at the calm lake that now had no signs of the whirlpool. Fez and Tink looked at her with blank stares.

"Who?" Tink asked.

"Charybdis," Ellie repeated. "She's a sea monster that makes giant whirlpools just by inhaling. Maybe she has been doing that and sucking up the jellyfish."

"Maybe," said Tink. "But this is a lake, not a sea."

"She visits lakes, too," Ellie explained. "I know Charybdis comes here because I see her in paparazzi photos on this beach all the

time. And look by my foot: this big long tooth is exactly like hers."

Fez squinted at the long, smooth fang lying on the beach. "You sure that's a tooth?"

"Of course!" said Ellie. She picked it up. "Just look how strong it is." She bent the tooth and it snapped in half, revealing splinters of wood.

"Or, it could be smooth beach wood," Tink said.

Ellie frowned. "Okay, that wasn't a tooth, but the whirlpool still sounds like Charybdis."

"Alright, so what kind of evidence would we need to prove that it was Charybdis?" Tink asked.

Ellie looked around the lake and thought.

"None," Fez said, to everyone's surprise.

Ellie slammed her eyebrows together. "Fez, a good detective *always* needs evidence. How else are we going to prove it?"

Fez unzipped Tink's backpack.

"Hey, what are you doing?" Tink asked.

"I know I put it in here somewhere," said Fez, reaching into the backpack. "Ah ha!" Fez yanked out a magazine.

"Um, that's not mine," Tink said.

"I know!" exclaimed Fez. "You always have your backpack, so sometimes I store things in there. I put this cooking magazine in just in case I wanted to read on the beach today."

"You just store stuff in my backpack!?"

"Yuppers!" Fez said with a huge grin.

Ellie giggled. "That's smart. But is now really the time to find a new recipe?"

Fez flipped through the magazine and finally stopped at a page near the back.

"No, look!" he said. Right there in the gossip section was a picture of Charybdis lying on a beach in Hawaii with her sunglasses and straw hat, sipping a fruit smoothie.

Ellie looked at the date on the photo. "That's only two days ago," Ellie calculated.

"Not nearly enough time to make it to Jellyfish Lake."

"Exactly!" exclaimed Fez. "I thought I saw that funny name somewhere recently. Did you know she has her own line of blenders?" Fez reached over to put his magazine back in the backpack, but Tink pulled away.

Tink squinted at Fez.

"Sorry, I'll ask next time," Fez assured Tink.

"Next time!?"

"Guys, I think we have something bigger to concentrate on than backpacks," Ellie exclaimed. She pointed to the giant footprints in the sand that led to the side of the lake. "I looked all over for footprints today and there is no way I would have missed ones this big. They must be new."

"Do you see what I see?" asked Tink.

"Of course, I'm the one that pointed out the footprints," Ellie said, a little annoyed he was trying to take credit. "Weren't you listening?"

"No, where they lead," Tink clarified. He raced to the thick oak tree and found a wooden cogwheel that blended in with the tree's trunk.

"If I am not mistaken..." Tink turned the cog by the handle, and the water started swirling, "I would say that this creates the whirlpools."

CLUNK!

The wheel stopped. Tink tried to continue turning it, but it was stuck.

"Oh well," he said. "We know what it does." He let go and wiped his hands on his pants.

"That's a great find!" complimented Ellie. "How did you spot that?"

"I could see the metal wire shining in the moonlight," Tink explained.

Ellie frowned. "I completely missed that..." She let out a heavy breath. "Maybe Jack is right and I will never be a real detective. How could I miss that?"

"Don't listen to Jack," insisted Fez. "He's just a big bully."

Ellie laughed, then reached in her trench coat pocket and pulled out her notebook. "Funny you should say that!" she said as she flipped to the page she had been working on earlier. She tapped on where she'd written about Jack being a bully.

1. ~~Pollution~~ – *(The water tested fine and the frog wasn't dead.)*
2. ~~Jack~~ – *(The jellyfish went missing before he arrived. But he's still a big bully!)*
3. *Someone that needs the jellyfish for something… but who?*

Ellie ran her finger over the last line of her notebook entry. That was it!

"I think someone used the cogwheel to steal the jellyfish!" Ellie exclaimed. "We just have to figure out who." She turned her attention to the footprints. "These turn and go toward the forest. I bet if we follow them, we can find the jellyfish thief."

Chapter Nine
Cabin in the Woods

Ellie, Tink, and Fez followed the giant footsteps to an old cabin not too far into the woods. All three of them stood at the warped wood door, bugs crawling about the nooks and crannies. Ellie watched a spider scurry by, plucked it off, and popped it in her mouth.

CRUNCH! CRUNCH!

"That will never not gross me out," Tink said with a gag. They peered into a window beside the door, but there were no lights, and the window was caked with filth. They couldn't see anything.

CREAK! Fez had his hand on the door, and both Ellie and Tink shushed him at the same time.

"Sorry," Fez whispered. "But the door wasn't even shut." After one last look in the dirty window, they decided to go in. The floorboards squeaked and creaked as they tiptoed through the door into the small one-room cabin. They shone their flashlights around to find furniture covered in white sheets that had turned grey from filth and shelves of books covered in layers of thick dust. The air felt heavy with the stench of molded wood and mothballs.

"Looks like it's abandoned," Tink whispered. A brown rat ran across the floor with a small squeak. "Well, almost abandoned."

"It's so cute!" Fez declared, trying to find exactly where it had run to.

Ellie shuddered as the critter scurried under the desk in the corner. She had an urge to bolt out of the cabin, but she knew they needed to solve this mystery to save Jellyfish Lake. She picked up an old magnifying glass off a small wooden table and blew the dust off. She raised it to her face and squinted at the room through the lens. She loved how big everything appeared through a magnifying glass. The rat ran to the other side of the room, and it looked like a giant monster, making Ellie jump.

"Do you think that maybe that bus driver just saw a rat or other rodent on the road?" asked Ellie after some thought.

"A giant rat?" asked Tink.

"No, a normal-sized one. But maybe it just

looked huge through his thick glasses. Like looking through a magnifying glass." Ellie placed the magnifying glass back on the table.

"Maybe," said Tink. "But if that's the case, I really hope he isn't our driver on the way home."

Ellie was looking at Fez trying to lure the rat out from a crack in the wall when she spotted something. The rat left behind little footprints on the dirty floor wherever it ran. She shone her flashlight behind her. She was leaving footprints too—the floor was that dirty. However, there was one path on the floor that was almost like a trail. It had much less dirt. As if the dust was worn away.

Ellie followed the trail to a bookshelf. There were lots of odd little knick-knacks like porcelain clowns, trinket boxes, and toy cars scattered among the many books. As she scanned the dozen shelves, one trinket box stood out from the rest. It wasn't anything special, just a silver heart with a rose on top, but it was the only thing on the whole shelf that wasn't dusty. Ellie tried to lift the box, but it wouldn't budge,

so instead, she opened it. Inside was a red button. She took a deep breath and jabbed it with her finger. The bookcase beside her swung open with a thump. Fez and Tink both turned.

"How did you do that!?" Tink asked.

Ellie gave a big fanged smile. She couldn't believe she did it.

"Do you guys remember the episode of *The Amazing Vampire Detective* when Hailey Haddie

found the diamonds?" Fez and Tink nodded, so Ellie continued. "She found them because the book that opened the hiding spot was the only thing that didn't have dust on it." Ellie pointed to the box before waving for them to go with her through the door.

The trio peered into the secret passageway and found a dimly lit staircase going down.

Ellie gulped. "You two first," she whispered.

"Why do we have to go first?" Fez complained.

"Because I found the hidden door."

The two boys couldn't argue with that, so they stepped down the first few stairs, followed by Ellie, and one very unexpected guest. To Fez's delight, the rat that they had seen earlier followed them onto the stairs. Fez let out a tiny squeal when he spotted the little critter. He wanted to be friends with every animal he met.

Fez ran back up the stairs, passed Ellie, and managed to corner the rat on one of the steps.

"Don't worry, little guy, I don't want to hurt you," he assured his new furry friend as he

scooped him off the wooden step. "Oh, that's a cute sweater. Wait… why are you wearing a leopard-print sweater?"

ACHOO!

"Sanalamia, Fez," said Ellie as she squinted to try to see what might be at the bottom of the stairs.

"Umm, that wasn't me," said Fez. Ellie and Tink turned around to see Jessica in Fez's arms.

Chapter Ten
Rat, Bat, Cat, or Worm

"Jessica!?" Ellie cried. "Where did you come from?"

"And how did you just appear?" Tink added.

Jessica hopped out of Fez's arms, and the secret door slammed shut. Her leopard-print sweater had caught on a red lever. "Oops," Jessica said with a quivering lip as she unhooked her sweater. Tink ran up the stairs and lifted the lever, but the door didn't budge. All Ellie could do was stand on the stairs with her mouth open. She couldn't believe her eyes.

"This isn't reopening the door!" Tink cried, giving it one last tug.

"Forget about that!" Ellie snapped. "Where

did you come from?" she asked Jessica once again.

"I got my transformational powers. And can you guess what I am?" Jessica's eyes filled with tears. "I couldn't be something cool and classic like a bat, I had to be— I had to be,—"

Ellie gasped. "You're a rat!"

Jessica burst into tears. "I'm a gross brown rat. And now you won't want to be my friend anymore. I tried being mean to you so you wouldn't want to be friends and would never have to find out, but now you know." Jessica sat down on the step, put her head in her hands, and sobbed. Ellie walked up the steps and gave her best friend a hug.

"Jess, I will always be your friend. I don't care if you're a rat. I'm actually excited, because now we get to deal with transformational powers together."

Jessica sniffled. "But how can you be my friend if you're scared of me? You're scared of everything."

Ellie giggled. "Well, yeah, I'm scared of a lot, but I could never be scared of you." Ellie

thought back to earlier, when the rat that was presumably Jessica had run across her foot. "Earlier at the beach, I was just startled," Ellie explained. "I'll always be your friend. Whether you're a rat, bat, cat, or worm."

Jessica's eyes widened. "Oh, thank goodness I am not a worm!" Both girls laughed.

"Do you guys still want to be my friend, even if I'm a gross rat?" asked Jessica with a lip tremble as she turned to Fez and Tink.

"Dude, I think that's awesome!" said Fez. "You're adorable as a rat!"

Jessica stood and put her hand on her hips. "Are you saying I'm not adorable as a vampire?"

Fez's face dropped. "No… I just think animals are extra cute."

"I have a question," announced Tink.

Jessica groaned. "No, I can't control it. For some reason, sneezes seem to trigger the transformation. I guess kind of like being scared triggers it for Ellie. But unlike her, I can't turn into a rat or vampire on command. Only when I sneeze. Then once I'm a rat, I have to sneeze again to turn back."

"Actually, I was going to ask, if I build a rat maze in the lab, will you test-run it for me?" Tink said in a soft voice.

"No! Absolutely not," Jessica bellowed as she threw her hands in the air.

Tink looked at Fez and shrugged. "It was worth a try."

"Thanks, guys," Jessica said with a smile. "Does this mean we can solve this mystery now?"

They all cheered.

They walked down the stairs and found themselves in a large cave with flickers of blue light dancing on the walls. Right in the middle, there was a large pool of turquoise water. The water was moving, and soon it became clear what the deep pool contained.

"The jellyfish!" Fez cried. "Look how cute and squidgy they are."

"There must be thousands of them here," Jessica added.

"We did it!" said Tink with a fist pump in the air. The four friends high-fived and it echoed throughout the cave. Then they all put their fingers to their lips. "Shhh!"

"But who is behind this?" Jessica asked. "I was worried about you guys, so I've been following you as a rat since Fez made me sneeze

by blowing dirt at me from ground beef jerky." She squinted at Fez.

"It was Jelly Belly Liver Jam Jerky. NOT beef jerky," Fez corrected.

"Either way, it was dirty ground jerky. Anyway, my point is, I know you followed some big footprints from the beach. Do you think whoever those footprints belong to stole the jellyfish?"

"Yes, but that's all we know," Ellie confirmed. Ellie wandered to a corner of the cave with papers stuck to the wall. There was a fridge running off a generator in the corner and a bunch of bowls, jars, and spoons spread out across a counter.

"Come here," she told everyone. She pointed to a recipe taped to the wall titled *Secret Recipe*. There were lots of ingredients scratched out in black ink.

"You're the food expert," Ellie said to Fez. "What do you think?" Ellie opened the fridge and found dozens of jars of jam. But not just any jam: glowing jam.

Fez scratched his chin. "Seems to be some

sort of weird jam. But who makes jam with jellyfish?"

"I do!" came a loud voice from behind them.

The friends whirled around to see a ginormous furry creature emerge from the pool of water. The wet brown fur that covered his entire eight-foot-tall body dripped onto his giant feet. They had finally found the jellyfish thief—and he was much bigger than any of them had imagined.

POOF!

Chapter Eleven
Jelly Belly

"Hey, you guys look familiar," said the humongous furry monster. "Aren't you that little detective team that saved the Royal Wedding?"

Tink, Fez, and Jessica silently nodded.

POOF! Ellie transformed back into a vampire and nodded as well.

"Neat trick!" the creature said. He walked toward the group and held out his hand. "I'm Bigfoot, pleased to meet you!" One by one, they all shook his ginormous thumb.

"Gee, you guys sure are quiet now," Bigfoot said. "You were a lot louder when you had your whole rat conversation on the stairs."

"Hey, that was a private conversation!" Jessica exclaimed.

"Ah, so you guys do still talk," Bigfoot said.

"We're just kind of shocked," Tink said. "I didn't think you existed."

Bigfoot patted down his wet fur. "Last time I checked, I did."

Tink gave a small smile.

"I knew you existed," said Ellie, "but I never expected you to be able to talk."

Bigfoot let out a laugh that boomed and echoed through the cave. "Fair enough; I know there are a lot of weird stories about me. The worst is probably that one where the lady makes soup with my toe."

"Wait, that was true!?" Fez asked.

"Kind of. I did lose my big toe, but no woman found it and ate it. A good lesson to be careful with an ax, though." Bigfoot chuckled. "I guess you could say I had an ax-ccident." Everyone giggled this time. While Bigfoot was nothing like any of them had imagined, they could all agree he was really friendly, and quite funny.

Ellie thought back to the footsteps and didn't

remember a toe missing. She looked down at his big hairy feet and counted ten toes.

"If you lost a toe, why do you have ten?" Ellie questioned.

Bigfoot reached down and, with a small pop, pulled off his big toe.

"This one is just a prosthetic! I am quite

the craftsman when it comes to putting things together. Well, except recipes, apparently."

"That's because you're not supposed to put cute and squishy jellyfish in jam!" Fez scolded.

"I actually haven't yet. I've tried everything but can't get the recipe exactly right. The release of Jelly Belly Glowing Jelly is next month, and I figured jellyfish were squishy, so maybe they would work."

Fez's jaw dropped. "You're behind Jelly Belly Liver Jam Jerky!?"

"Sure am!" said Bigfoot, rubbing his stomach. "Who else has a jelly belly like me?" He gave his stomach a shake, and it jiggled like a bowl of gelatin.

"I LOVE your jerky," gushed Fez.

"Glad you like it. That fridge back there has a whole shelf at the bottom, so help yourself," offered Bigfoot. Fez's eyes grew wide, and he gladly accepted.

"You need to release these jellyfish back into the lake," Ellie told Bigfoot. "If you don't, they are going to have to close the park."

"And cancel the summer camp!" Tink added.

"Oh my, I had no idea," said Bigfoot. "But I need the jellyfish for my jelly." He turned back to look at the pool's flickering blue water.

"What if we could fix your jam without using the jellyfish?" asked Jessica.

"Then that would be a deal!" said Bigfoot.

"While you're at it, you should change your packaging," Ellie added. "Your wrappers are all over the beach."

"Noted," Bigfoot said. "I am actually working on compostable packaging."

"Great!" exclaimed Ellie. "Then let's do this so we can go back to our cabins."

Bigfoot opened the fridge and retrieved a bright blue jar of jam with a blackberry label.

"This one has plenty of glow, but it tastes kind of funny," Bigfoot explained. He unscrewed the lid and handed everyone a spoon. The whole gang slurped up their spoonful and then made faces like they'd just sucked on lemons.

"Why is it so sour!?" Fez asked through puckered cheeks.

"The solution I use to make it glow turns everything sour and bitter." Bigfoot yanked

open a drawer and pulled out a small vial of Neo Glo. Jessica opened the Neo Glo and took a sniff.

"Ick! I can see why," Jessica announced. "Smells like rotten limes and stinky cheese." She handed it to Tink, who scanned the ingredient list.

"Did you try putting more sugar in the recipe?" Fez asked.

"Sure did," Bigfoot said. "Still wasn't good." Bigfoot grabbed another jar from the fridge. This one also had a blackberry label but was more of a dark purple color. Once again, everyone took a bite, but this time they instantly spit it out. Bigfoot groaned. "So, it is as bad as I think."

"Possibly worse," said Jessica as she wiped her tongue on her arm.

"How does that glow stuff make everything taste so bad?" Ellie asked.

Bigfoot looked at the floor, then the ceiling. "Um, well, that one doesn't even have the Neo Glo. That was my base recipe…"

Ellie's face turned bright red. "I just meant that it has a very unique taste."

Bigfoot laughed. "No, it tastes awful. I just can't figure out how to make good jam consistently. Even the batches that turn out okay get ruined with the taste of Neo Glo."

"What if I could isolate the glow and take out some of the bitter taste?" Tink inquired as he looked over the Neo Glo ingredients.

"That would be awesome!" said Bigfoot. "But it won't make the bad batches of jam good."

"No, but we know someone who is a great cook," said Ellie.

"Someone who could teach you," Jessica added. Everyone looked toward Fez, who was now digging in the fridge. He closed the door and found everyone silently staring at him.

"Me?" Fez asked.

"Of course!" said Ellie.

"Oh! I would be happy to help!" Fez said as he unwrapped a stick of jerky. "But as soon as I get the taste of the last jelly out of my mouth."

Everyone agreed that was a great idea.

After a quick snack, hours of cooking, and a pile of dishes almost as tall as Bigfoot, they did it! They had a glowing jam. It didn't taste sour. It didn't taste bad. In fact, it tasted amazing. Like a bowl of ripe berries sprinkled with sugar.

"Thank you so much!" said Bigfoot. "I owe you guys big time."

"No problem," Ellie said. "This has been a lot of fun!" Everyone nodded in agreement. "We should get going, though," Ellie added with a yawn.

"We should definitely go," Tink agreed. "It must be really late!"

"Umm, just one problem," said Bigfoot as everyone started for the stairs. "We are kind of trapped in here."

"What do you mean?" asked Ellie.

"You guys sure do like to touch things. When you hit the red lever on the stairs, you put the place on lockdown. That usually wouldn't be a problem, but you also turned that cogwheel on the tree and jammed the emergency exit in

the pool that leads to the lake. I could only pry it open a crack."

"We're stuck?" asked Jessica.

Bigfoot nodded. "We're stuck."

Chapter Twelve
Ready Yeti

They were stuck in a cave with Bigfoot. If they couldn't get out, they would be in big trouble when their teacher discovered they were missing. And it may be too late for Jellyfish Lake.

"Isn't there a way to undo the lockdown?" Tink asked in disbelief.

"Nope," said Bigfoot. "It's a fairly new system, so it still has some kinks."

Jessica looked at the pool that contained the jellyfish and the small work area.

"What on earth would you need a lockdown for? If someone steals back the jellyfish? There isn't much in here."

Bigfoot squinted. "Yeti."

"Yeti?" all four asked in unison.

"Wait, isn't that just another name for you?" Fez asked.

"No!" Bigfoot roared. "I am so tired of people thinking I am the same as that—as that furry fraud. I am smart enough to make my own snack creations, but him, well..." Bigfoot exhaled hard. "He is always trying to rip me off. Like his newest product, 'Ready Yeti Kidney Jam Jerky.'" Bigfoot grunted. "Clearly a huge rip-off!" He let out a roar of frustration that shook the cave. The detective squad backed away from the furry beast.

"Sorry," Bigfoot apologized, as they stared at him wide-eyed. "I just can't stand him and how he treats me." Bigfoot took a deep breath. "I know it's best not to let him get to me and to ignore his shenanigans. But it's hard sometimes. He really knows how to push my buttons! Surely, you know someone like that and understand."

Jack flashed through Ellie's mind—she knew all too well.

Ellie changed the topic. "Okay, but we need to get out of here soon, or we'll be in a lot of

trouble, and a bunch of people will be very worried."

Bigfoot shrugged. "Sorry, little vampire, the emergency exit is jammed, so there is only a tiny crack." Bigfoot scratched his chin. "However… If I pry it open a little more, someone small could fit through. Then, if they go back to the bookcase and push the button, we could all get out."

Ellie looked at Tink, who was clearly the smallest out of the five of them. "Looks like you have some swimming to do."

Bigfoot shook his head. "No, the opening is much smaller than him… more like, oh, I don't know. Bat-sized."

A lump settled in Ellie's throat. There was no way she was swimming in that deep water, especially with all those jellyfish. "Jessica's a rat!" she blabbed, trying to pass off the task.

"Ellie, I can only transform when I sneeze," Jessica said with a sigh.

Ellie frantically grabbed some dirt off the ground and threw it at Jessica.

"Ellie!" Jessica shrieked. "What are you

doing?" Jessica grabbed some dirt and threw it back.

Ellie coughed and stuck out her tongue. "I was just trying to get you to sneeze."

"I can't do this for you," Jessica said as she shook the dirt out of her red curls and wiped her hands on her dress. "Only you can. Just think of how much trouble we are going to be in if we don't get out of here and how sad Hailey Haddie would be if her favorite vacation spot closed—"

"And about my Science Camp!" Tink interrupted.

"And yes, Tink's Science Camp," Jessica repeated. She looked over at Tink. "I was getting there."

"But I don't think I can do it," Ellie said in a small voice. Ellie kicked a small pebble, and it skipped across the cave floor. Her stomach felt like it had hundreds of butterflies fluttering around in it.

"What if we swim with you as far as we can?" Jessica offered as she took Ellie's hand and gave it a squeeze.

Ellie looked up at her three best friends, all nodding in agreement. When she went on this field trip, she'd expected to have fun and maybe meet Hailey Haddie—if she was lucky—not to have the fate of Jellyfish Lake depend on her. She took in a deep breath, puffed out her cheeks, and blew out a big exhale. If there was ever a time to prove she was more than a Scaredy Bat, it was now.

"Okay," Ellie finally agreed. "Let's do this."

Chapter Thirteen
Little Ballerinas

Ellie stood at the edge of the pool filled with jellyfish and watched them gently gliding around the water.

"Are you sure they can't hurt me?" Ellie asked for the fifth time.

"Positive!" Tink reassured her. "The fact that this type of jellyfish doesn't sting is what makes Jellyfish Lake so popular."

Ellie rubbed the goosebumps on her arms. "Alright, then let's get this over with."

Bigfoot went over the plan one more time. "I am going to pry open the door; then I need you guys to jam my fake toe in it to make sure it doesn't close before Ellie is out." He reached down to his massive furry foot, popped off his

fake big toe once again, and offered it to Jessica.

"No way!" Jessica squealed, putting her hands behind her back.

Fez gladly grabbed the giant toe. "This is so cool," he declared. With the toe firmly placed under his arm, he lined up on the water's edge with everyone else.

"Ready?" shouted Bigfoot. "Five, four, three…"

Ellie took the deepest breath she could and clenched her eyes shut.

"Two, one."

SPLASH!

The chill of the water enveloped her whole body. All she could see was blackness, but then she remembered her eyes were still shut. She opened them and things started coming into focus. Everyone was swimming toward the bottom of the pool. Jellyfish swam around each side of her, and a bright pink one circled her head before gliding down and tickling her leg with its tentacles. Ellie gave a small smile. The smack of jellyfish looked like little ballerinas

moving in slow motion, with their wispy tentacles waving about and the gentle sway of their bodies—they were beautiful.

Ellie looked down at Jessica, waving at her to come to the bottom of the pool. She was surprised when she found herself wishing she could stay longer with the jellyfish. Multiple jellyfish brushed against her as she swam to the bottom.

She arrived just in time. Bigfoot pried open the metal door so Fez could jam the big toe in.

TUNK!

The door slammed down over the toe, leaving a tiny opening. Ellie got a big hairy thumbs-up and knew this was her moment.

POOF!

She transformed into a bat, flapped her wings, and zipped through the small opening into the weedy bottom of the lake. Ellie's bat wings made great flippers—she was able to propel herself around quicker than usual.

Just breathe, she reminded herself. *No, wait! Don't do that! You'll inhale water. Just relax and keep flapping.*

She zigged and zagged through the weedy bottom until the light of the moon was visible. Quickly, she started flapping to the surface, but she wasn't going anywhere. A weed had wrapped itself around her leg and was keeping her at the bottom of the lake.

She reached down to try to untangle herself, but her small bat hands were no use.

This can't be happening! Why didn't I pay more attention when my Dad taught me about tying and untying knots? she silently fretted.

Next, she tried to transform back into a vampire, but it didn't work. She needed to concentrate on transforming, and she was panicking too much. The air in her lungs was quickly disappearing. A few bubbles escaped her mouth as she gave a big tug.

Jellyfish swam around her as she frantically tried to free her foot, but none seemed to notice her struggle. Until the bright pink one appeared. It wrapped its tentacles under the weed and, with one big tug, Ellie was finally free. She flew to the surface and rocketed out of the water into the night sky.

The fresh forest air never felt so good.

Chapter Fourteen
Wishes And Dreams

The four friends sat on the cool beach sand and watched the sun creep over the horizon.

"And then after I made it out of the water, getting to the button to open the door for you guys was no problem," Ellie explained as she tried to stifle a yawn.

Jessica gasped. "I can't believe you got stuck! Are you sure you're okay?"

"Yeah, I'm sure," Ellie reassured her. "I was lucky that jellyfish was there to help me, though. I had no idea they were so smart."

"But they're not really," said Tink. "Don't get me wrong, they're fascinating creatures,

but understanding someone is in danger and helping, well, that is just odd."

"Not as odd as Jessica being a rat." Fez pointed to the rat-shaped birthmark on Jessica's arm and gave it a poke. "Look how cute it is," he teased. Jessica covered the spot with her hand and narrowed her eyes at him.

"Alright, explain this to me one more time," said Tink.

Jessica threw her head back. "Ellie, I can't explain this again, it's your turn."

Ellie smiled at the thought of Jessica already explaining this to the boys three times. "Okay, so some vampires have birthmarks that show which animal they transform into. But the birthmark only appears once their transformational powers kick in."

"It's not technically a birthmark if you haven't had it since you were born," scoffed Tink.

"It looks like one, so that's what it's called," Ellie explained. "I don't make the rules. Anyway, I don't have one because my dad is human and only full vampires get them."

"And this is a big secret?" Fez asked.

"Yes. When vampires weren't accepted, often we would transform into our animal form to hide. My parents said humans still don't know we can turn into other animals besides bats. And they definitely don't know full vampires have marks that show what animal they transform into," explained Ellie.

"It's a big secret because our transformations are what will keep us safe in case we ever have to go into hiding again," Jessica added. "So you can't tell anyone!"

"We won't," promised both boys.

Ellie looked back at the calm lake. A woodpecker tapped against a tree not too far away.

"I can't believe I did it," she said with a small smile as she thought about the crazy night they'd had. She looked over at her three best friends. "I can't believe *we* did it," she corrected.

With their help, Bigfoot had figured out how to make his glowing jelly taste great—all without using jellyfish. So, he promised to release all the jellyfish and sort everything out with the park rangers. Jellyfish Lake was saved thanks to the little detective team.

Even though they couldn't tell anyone about their adventure without getting in heaps of trouble for sneaking out, they were happy to keep the experience between them. Ellie was thrilled to have solved another mystery, while Jessica was simply content to have her friends

by her side. Fez was enthusiastically munching on the unlimited supply of Jelly Belly Liver Jam Jerky Bigfoot offered as thanks for helping with the recipe. And Tink, well, Tink may have been the most excited of all. He couldn't stop talking about how Bigfoot offered him a spot at the Jellyfish Lake Science Camp.

It turned out that Bigfoot reserved a few camp spots every year for kids that his company sponsored. And after talking to Tink about the science behind Jelly Belly's recipes, he knew Tink deserved a spot.

"I just can't believe I get to go to Science Camp!" Tink squealed.

"We know, we know," said Jessica. "Can't you talk about anything else?"

"No way!" exclaimed Tink. "You're going to be hearing about this forever. This is my dream come true."

Jessica groaned, and Ellie chuckled. Just as Ellie thought nothing could ruin the bliss she felt, a familiar voice came from behind her.

"Aw, is Scaredy Bat and her wannabe detective squad too scared to go swimming?" Jack

taunted. With a cackle, he threw his bag down and ran into the lake.

Ellie balled her hands into fists by her side.

"I am getting so sick of him!" she exploded. "I wish he really would turn purple."

"Don't let him get to you," Jessica said. "Bigfoot was right. We should just ignore him when he's trying to bother us."

Ellie knew she was right, but sometimes that felt impossible.

A few minutes later, the sun was fully out, and Jack ran back to shore and popped his sunscreen out of his bag. He began slathering the thick lotion over his face, and to Ellie's surprise—and delight—it was purple!

Ellie's mouth dropped open as Jack's face turned the color of a grape. He started rubbing more on his arms and then looked down.

"What is this!?" he cried, looking at the purple goop. Jack glared at Tink. "Did you do this?"

Tink shook his head.

Jack tried to wipe his hands on his swim trunks, but they were stained purple. He ran

back into the lake and frantically splashed water over his face and arms, but nothing happened. Jack came out of the lake, huffing and puffing.

"Mr. Bramble!" he cried as he ran to the cabins.

"Tink, you're a genius!" Jessica laughed.

"It really wasn't me this time!" exclaimed Tink.

Ellie giggled. "I guess some wishes do come true."

Fez shut his eyes. "I wish for a pet llama." He opened his eyes and looked around the beach, but there was no llama in sight. He slumped his shoulders. "It was worth a try."

Ellie hopped to her feet. "You guys ready?" Everyone else followed, and they raced into the lake. But after only a few minutes of splashing and playing, Ellie got her necklace caught in her hair.

"Be right back!" Ellie called to her friends as she rushed to shore. Her chain was wrapped around a big chunk of her hair. Ellie tugged on it, but it was really twisted in there.

A sloshing sound came from the shore, and Ellie caught a glimpse of pink from Jessica's swimsuit coming out of the water.

"Jess, can you help me?" Ellie asked. Jessica came over and helped her untangle the necklace. Once the purple dragon pendant was safely in her bag, Ellie turned around to thank Jessica. But it wasn't Jessica at all.

Ellie gasped. It was Hailey Haddie!

Hailey gave a small wave and smiled as she walked past. Too shocked to form words, all Ellie could do was watch her hero walk up the beach. And that was when she saw it. The jellyfish-shaped birthmark on Hailey Haddie's ankle.

Chapter Fifteen
An Invitation

*D*ear *Ellie,*
I know all the work you did to save Jellyfish Lake and I can't thank you enough! It is the one place in the world I can go to "blend in" and be normal for a while. I don't know what I would do without it, and I don't know what the world would do without budding detectives like you—you and your friends make a great team!

Speaking of detective work, I know on the beach that you noticed my birthmark, and I beg you and your friends… please don't tell anyone. I'm counting on you to keep my biggest secret.

I would like to invite you all to my movie filming in Brookside next month to thank you personally. The set passes are enclosed. In the meantime, I thought

you might enjoy an advance copy of my latest book.

See you on set!

With love and gratitude,

Hailey Haddie

Ellie's hand shook, causing the letter to tremble like a leaf as she read it out loud to her friends. She couldn't believe it. Not only did her all-time hero Hailey Haddie know she existed, but Hailey also sent her a personal letter, an advance copy of her book, *and* an invitation to go on set. Ellie's mouth gaped, and her heart hammered against her chest.

"Did Hailey Haddie just invite us all to her movie set?" Jessica asked in disbelief.

Tink nodded. "It would seem she did."

Ellie let out a loud squeal and began dancing around and singing, "I'm going to see Hailey Haddie again! I'm going to see Hailey Haddie again!"

Jessica put her hands on her hips and loudly cleared her throat.

Ellie paused for a couple of seconds, looked at her friends, and then restarted her song and dance. "*We're* going to see Hailey Haddie.

We're going to see Hailey Haddie!" Jessica, Tink, and Fez joined in. They hopped around the room, fantasizing about what being on the movie set would be like and disagreeing on what the best part would be.

"I hear they have a great special effects department," said Tink.

"Ooo, movie sets always have the best food!"

said Fez with a glimmer of excitement in his eye.

"Oh, Fez." Jessica let out a short giggle. "I can't wait to visit the costume department. It's always my favorite part of visiting my mom's movie sets." She smiled at Ellie. "What are you the most excited about?"

Everyone laughed, because they knew that question needed no answer.

While the four friends were excited about their set invitation for different reasons, they could all agree on one thing—it was going to be a blast.

Everyone left shortly after, and Ellie lay on her pink coffin bed with Hailey Haddie's book, *How to Be the World's Greatest Detective: A Step-by-Step Guide to Solving Mysteries*. But before she could crack it open, her pesky sister Penny sauntered in.

"Whatcha reading, Scaredy Bat?" Penny asked.

"Get out of my room!" Ellie shouted.

"Okay," said Penny, to Ellie's surprise. Then she grabbed the book and ran.

"Get back here, you little brat," Ellie screamed. She caught up to Penny at the end of the hall, tackled her to the ground, and snatched the book.

"Ow! I'm telling Mom!" Penny threatened. "And I saw what you were reading. A Scaredy Bat like you will never be a real detective." With a quivering lip, Penny ran downstairs. "Mom! Ellie jumped on me!"

Ellie took in a deep breath and made her way back into her room, this time making sure to close the door. But as she climbed back on her bed with her book, her excitement wasn't the same. What Penny had said was much like the words Jack taunted her with—that Scaredy Bats couldn't be real detectives. She thought of the mysteries she'd solved, but what if those didn't count? She ran her finger over the title of the book and figured it was as good a place as any to start building her detective skills.

She cracked the thick book open to the first page and took a deep inhale of the fresh pages. She knew she would cherish this book forever, but the inscription on the second page

scribbled in gold ink was just the icing on the cake.

Ellie,

"Great detectives aren't born; they're made. May this book help you become the best you can be... And never forget, believing in yourself goes a long way."

Hailey Haddie

Being a Scaredy Bat certainly wasn't always easy, but Ellie knew she was doing her best. As for proving she was a real detective, well, that could wait until another day.

Hi!

Did you enjoy the mystery?

I know I did!

If you want to join the team as we solve more mysteries, then leave a review!

Otherwise, we won't know if you're up for the next mystery. And when we go to solve it, you may never get to hear about it!

You can **leave a review** wherever you found the book.

The gang and I are excited to see you in the next mystery adventure!

Fingers crossed there's nothing scary in that one...

Don't miss
Book #4 in the

Scaredy Bat

series!

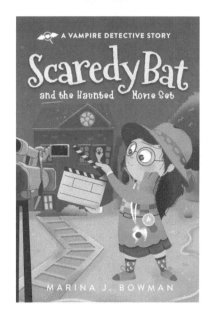

Learn more at:
scaredybat.com/bundle1

Do you want to be a detective?

Get your FREE Custom Detective Guide to become the sleuth you were born to be!

GO HERE TO GET YOUR
DETECTIVE GUIDE NOW:

scaredybat.com/bundle1

Are You Afraid of Deep Water?

Thalassophobia [thah-lah-sow-fow-bee-uh] is the intense and persistent fear of deep, dark bodies of water such as the ocean. It comes from "thalassa," the Greek word for sea and "phobos," the Greek word for fear.

Fear Rating: Thalassophobia is one of the somewhat common phobias. People with this phobia can experience a racing heart, rapid breathing, sweating, nausea, and dizziness.

Origin: Fear of deep water comes from an instinctual evolutionary response, a traumatic past experience, the unknown depths, and media portrayals.

Fear Facts:

- Water creatures are more afraid of you or have no interest (even sharks).
- 95% of sea animals are invertebrates (no backbone) like jellyfish & shrimp.
- Slimy seaweed is a main ingredient in sushi, ice cream, shampoo, toothpaste and makeup. It also produces up to 70% of the world's oxygen.
- Humans are made to float! You can also bring a floaty for more buoyancy.
- Tips: practice in pools, bring friends, play games, and focus on the beauty.

Jokes: How do you make a shark laugh?
Tell a whale of a tale!

Fear No More! With some caution, deep bodies of water like oceans and lakes are safe and fun. But if you believe you suffer from thalassophobia and want help, talk to your parents or doctor about treatment options. For more fear facts, visit: scaredybat.com/bundle1.

Suspect List

Fill in the suspects as you read, and don't worry if they're different from Ellie's suspects. When you think you've solved the mystery, fill out the "who did it" section on the next page!

Name: Write the name of your suspect
Motive: Write the reason why your suspect might have committed the crime
Access: Write the time and place you think it could have happened
How: Write the way they could have done it
Clues: Write any observations that may support the motive, access, or how

Suspect 1

Draw below

Name:
Motive:
Access:
How:
Clues:

Suspect 2

Draw below

Name:
Motive:
Access:
How:
Clues:

Suspect 3

Draw below

Name:	
Motive:	
Access:	
How:	
Clues:	

Suspect 4

Draw below

Name:	
Motive:	
Access:	
How:	
Clues:	

Who Did It?

Now that you've identified all of your suspects, it's time to use deductive reasoning to figure out who actually committed the crime! Remember, the suspect must have a strong desire to commit the crime (or cause the accident) and the ability to do so.

For more detective fun, visit: scaredybat.com/bundle1

Name:	
Motive:	
Access:	
How:	
Clues:	

Hidden Details
Observation Sheet
-- Level One --

1. Where did Ellie and her classmates visit for their school trip?
2. What did the bus driver see that made him slam on the breaks?
3. What sticky substance did Ellie step in by the lake?
4. What "dead" creature did the kids find that was actually sleeping?
5. What supposed "clue" did Ellie find at night on the beach?
6. Whose footprints did Ellie, Fez, and Tink follow to the cabin in the woods?
7. With her new transformation powers, what kind of animal does Jessica turn into?
8. What did Bigfoot need the jellyfish for?
9. Who or what helped Ellie when she got tangled in seaweed as a bat?
10. What color did Jack mysteriously turn at the end of the story?

Hidden Details Observation Sheet
-- Level Two --

1. What is the name of the snack company that Ellie got her jerky from?
2. What prize did Mr. Bramble announce on the bus for the best project?
3. Who or what grabbed Ellie's ankle when they were sitting around the campfire?
4. What device created the whirlpool that sucked up the jellyfish?
5. What supernatural creature did Ellie suspect was taking the jellyfish?
6. Where did Ellie find the button to open the secret door behind the bookcase?
7. What was the rat wearing in the cabin in the woods?
8. What is the name of Jelly Belly's competitor business?
9. What did the kids use to prop open the emergency exit at the bottom of the pool?
10. What does Hailey have on her ankle?

Hidden Details
Observation Sheet
-- Level Three --

1. What is the title of the book Tink reads on the bus ride?
2. What historical treaty was signed on the beaches of Jellyfish Lake?
3. Who is Tink's hero?
4. What does Ellie say when someone sneezes?
5. When they hear the lake will have to close, what prize did Mr. Bramble announce instead?
6. What did Fez store in Tink's backpack that helped them clear Charybdis of the crime?
7. How did Bigfoot actually lose his toe?
8. Why doesn't Ellie have a bat shaped birthmark?
9. What did Fez wish for?
10. What is the title of the book Hailey gave to Ellie?

For more detective fun, visit:
scaredybat.com/bundle1

Level One Answers

1. Jellyfish Lake
2. A big furry monster
3. Orange soda
4. A frog
5. A tooth / beach wood
6. Bigfoot's
7. A brown rat
8. To make jam
9. A pink jellyfish / Hailey Haddie
10. Purple

Level Two Answers

1. Jelly Belly
2. Tickets to Science Camp
3. Jack
4. A wooden cogwheel
5. Charybdis
6. Silver heart shaped box with a rose on top
7. A leopard print sweater / Jessica's sweater
8. Ready Yeti
9. Bigfoot's prosthetic toe
10. A jellyfish birthmark

Level Three Answers

1. The Wonders of Jellyfish Lake
2. The Fang and Flesh Treaty
3. Bonnie Samson
4. Sanalamia
5. Mega Adventure Land amusement park
6. A cooking magazine
7. In an ax-ccident
8. Because her dad is human and only full vampires get them
9. A pet llama
10. How to Be the World's Greatest Detective: A Step-by-Step Guide to Solving Mysteries

Questions for Discussion

1. What did you enjoy about this book?
2. What are some of the themes of this story?
3. How did the characters use their strengths to solve the mystery together?
4. What is another way Ellie and her friends could have handled Jack's bullying?
5. What fears did the characters express in the book? When have you been afraid? How have you dealt with your fears?
6. What is your favorite snack food? Would you rather try Jam Jerky or Glowing Jelly?
7. Who is the hero you would like to meet?
8. What other books, shows, or movies does this story remind you of?
9. What do you think will happen in the next book in the series?
10. If you could talk to the author, what is one question you would ask her?

For more discussion questions, visit:
scaredybat.com/bundle1

Also by
Marina J. Bowman

THE LEGEND OF PINEAPPLE COVE

A fantasy-adventure series for kids with bravery, kindness, and friendship. If you like reimagined mythology and animal sidekicks, you'll love this legendary story!

To learn more, visit
thelegendofpineapplecove.com/sbb1

About the Author

Marina J. Bowman is a writer and explorer who travels the world searching for wildly fantastical stories to share with her readers. Ever since she was a child, she has been fascinated with uncovering long lost secrets and chasing the mythical, magical, and supernatural. For her current story, Marina is investigating a charming town in the northern US, where vampires and humans live in harmony.

Marina enjoys sailing, flying, and nearly all other forms of transportation. She never strays far from the ocean for long, as it brings her both inspiration and peace. She stays away from the spotlight to maintain privacy and ensure the more unpleasant secrets she uncovers don't catch up with her.

As a matter of survival, Marina nearly always communicates with the public through her representative, Devin Cowick. Ms. Cowick is an entrepreneur who shares Marina's passion for travel and creative storytelling and is the co-founder of Code Pineapple.

Marina's last name is pronounced baʊmən, and rhymes with "now then."

Made in United States
Troutdale, OR
10/17/2023